The Military Institutions of the Romans

by Flavius Vegetius Renatus

Translated by John Clarke

Must Have Books
503 Deerfield Place
Victoria, BC
V9B 6G5
Canada

ISBN 9781773236964

The Military Institutions of the Romans

[Epitoma rei militaris - 390 A.D]

by

Flavius Vegetius Renatus

[Translated by Lieutenant John Clarke - 1767]

Introduction - 1940

Preface to Book I

Book I : The Selection and Training of New Levies

- The Roman Discipline the Cause of Their Greatness
- The Selection of Recruits
- The Proper Age for Recruits
- Their Size
- Signs of Desirable Qualities
- The Trades Proper for New Levies
- The Military Mark
- Initial Training
- To Learn to Swim
- The Post Exercise
- Not to Cut, But to Thrust with the Sword
- The Drill Called Armatura
- The Use of Missile Weapons
- The Use of the Bow
- The Sling
- The Loaded Javelin
- To be Taught to Vault
- And To Carry Burdens
- The Arms of the Ancients
- Entrenched Camps
- Evolutions
- Monthly Marches
- Conclusion

Preface to Book II

Book II : The Organization of the Legion

- The Military Establishment
- The Difference between the Legions and Auxiliaries
- Causes of Decay of the Legion
- The Organization of the Legion</li>
- The Officers of the Legion
- The Praefect of the Workmen
- The Tribune of the Soldiers
- Centuries and Ensigns of the Foot
- Legionary Troops of Horse
- Drawing up a Legion in Order of Battle
- Names of Soldiers Inscribed on their Shields
- Records and Accounts
- Soldier's Deposits
- Promotion in the Legion
- Legionary Music
- The Drilling of the Troops
- Machines and Tools of the Legion

Preface to Book III

Book III : Dispositions for Action

- The Number which Should Compose an Army
- Means of Preserving it in Health
- Care to Provide Forage and Provisions
- Methods to Prevent Mutiny in an Army
- Marches in the Neighborhood of the Enemy
- Passages of Rivers
- Rules for Encamping an Army
- Motives for the Plan of Operations of a Campaign
- How to Manage Raw and Undisciplined Troops
- Preparations for a General Engagement
- The Sentiments of the Troops should be Determined before Battle
- The Choice of the Field of Battle
- Order of Battle
- Proper Distances and Intervals
- Disposition of the Cavalry
- Reserves
- The Post of the General and of the Second and Third in Command
- Maneuvers in Action
- Various Formations for Battle

- The Flight of an Enemy should not be Prevented, but Facilitated
- Manner of Conducting a Retreat
- Armed Chariots and Elephants
- Resources in Case of Defeat
- General Maxims

Introduction [1940]

The most influential military treatise in the western world from Roman times to the 19th Century was Vegetius' DE RE MILITARI. Its impressions on our own traditions of discipline and organization are everywhere evident.

The Austrian Field Marshal, Prince de Ligne, as late as 1770, called it a golden book and wrote: "A God, said Vegetius, inspired the legion, but for myself, I find that a God inspired Vegetius." Richard Coeur de Lion carried DE RE MILITARI everywhere with him in his campaigns, as did his father, Henry II of England. Around 1000 A. D. Vegetius was the favorite author of Foulques the Black, the able and ferocious Count of Anjou. Numerous manuscript copies of Vegetius circulated in the time of Charlemagne and one of them was considered a necessity of life by his commanders. A manuscript Vegetius was listed in the will of Count Everard de Frejus, about 837 A. D., in the time of Ludwig the Just.

In his Memoirs, Montecuculli, the conqueror of the Turks at St. Gotthard, wrote: "However, there are spirits bold enough to believe themselves great captains as soon as they know how to handle a horse, carry a lance at charge in a tournament, or as soon as they have read the precepts of Vegetius." Such was the reputation of Vegetius for a thousand years.

Manuscript copies dating from the 10th to the 15th centuries are extant to the number of 150. DE RE MILITARI was translated into English, French, and Bulgarian before the invention of printing. The first printed edition was made in Utrecht in 1473. It was followed in quick succession by editions in Cologne, Paris and Rome. It was first published in English by Caxton, from an English manuscript copy, in 1489.

Flavius Vegetius Renatus was a Roman of high rank. In some manuscripts he is given the title of count. Raphael of Volterra calls him a Count of Constantinople. Little is known of his life. It is apparent from his book that he had not had extensive practical experience as a soldier.. He states quite frankly that his purpose was to collect and synthesize from ancient manuscripts and regulations the military customs and wisdom that made ancient Rome great. According to his statement, his principal sources were Cato the Elder, Cornelius Celsus, Paternus, Frontinus, and the regulations and ordinances of Augustus, Trajan and Hadrian.

The Emperor Valentinian, to whom the book is dedicated, is believed to be the second emperor of that name. He evidently was not Valentinian I since his successor, Gratian, is named in the book. Between the reign of Valentinian II and Valentinian III, Rome was taken and burned by Alaric, King of the Goths, an event that unquestionably would have been mentioned had it occurred before the book was written. Vegetius mentions the defeat of the Roman armies by the Goths, but probably refers to the battle of Adrianople where Valens, the colleague of Valentinian I, was killed.

It is a paradox that DE RE MILITARI, which was to become a military bible for innumerable generations of European soldiers, was little used by the Romans for whom it was written. The decay of the Roman armies had progressed too far to be arrested by Vegetius' pleas for a return to the virtues of discipline and courage of the ancients. At the same time Vegetius' hope for a revival of the ancient organization of the legion was impracticable. Cavalry had adopted the armor of the foot soldier and was just commencing to become the principal arm of the military forces. The heavy armed foot-soldier, formerly the backbone of the legion, was falling a victim of his own weight and immobility, and the light-armed infantry, unable to resist the shock of cavalry, was turning more and more to missile weapons. By one of the strange mutations of history, when later the cross-bow and gun-powder deprived cavalry of its shock-power, the tactics of Vegetius again became ideal for armies, as they had been in the times from which he drew his inspiration.

Vegetius unceasingly emphasized the importance of constant drill and severe discipline and this aspect of his work was very tiresome to the soldiers of the middle ages, the feudal system lending itself but poorly to discipline. "Victory in war," he states in his opening sentence, "does not depend entirely upon numbers or mere courage; only skill and discipline will insure it." His first book is devoted to the selection, training and discipline of recruits. He insists upon the utmost meticulousness in drill. "No part of drill is more essential in action than for soldiers to keep their ranks with the greatest exactness." His description of the many arms which the Roman soldier was required to become expert in reminds one of the almost innumerable duties of the present day infantryman. Recruits were to be hardened so as to be able to march twenty miles in half a summer's day at ordinary step and twenty-four miles at quick step. It was the ancient regulation that practice marches of this distance must be made three times a month.

The second book deals with the organization and officers of the legion, the ancient system of promotion, and how to form the legion for battle. We find the Romans provided for soldier's deposits, just as is done in the American army today; that guard and duty rosters were kept in those days as now; and that the Roman system of guard duty is only slig.htly different from our manual for interior guard duty. The field music is described and is an ornamental progenitor of that in use in United States. The legion owed its success, according to Vegetius, to its arms and its machines, as well as to the bravery of its soldiers. The legion had fifty-five ballista for throwing darts and ten onagri, drawn by oxen, for throwing stones. Every legion carried its ponton equipment, "small boats hollowed out of a single piece of cimber, with long cables or chains to fasten them together." And in addition were "whatever is necessary for every kind of service, that the encampments may have all the strength and conveniences of a fortified city." Trains of workmen were provided to perform all the duties now performed by the various services in armies.

The third book deals with tactics and strategy and it was this portion of Vegetius that influenced war in the Middle Ages so greatly. He explains the use of reserves, attributing this invention to the Spartans, from whom the Romans adopted it. "It is much better to have several bodies of reserves than to extend your front too much" - an injunction as good today as when it was written. Encircling pursuit is described. The terrain is not overlooked. "The nature of the ground is often of more consequence than courage." The enemy should be estimated carefully. "It is essential to know the character of the enemy and of their principal officers-whether they be rash or cautious, enterprising or timid, whether they fight from careful calculation or from chance."

Vegetius' work is filled with maxims that have become a part of our everyday life. "He, therefore, who aspires to peace should prepare for war." "The ancients preferred discipline to numbers." "In the midst of peace, war is looked upon as an object too distant to merit consideration." "Few men are born brave; many become so through training and force of discipline."

Vegetius was a reformer who attempted to restore the degenerate Romans of the 4th Century to the military virtues of the ancients, whom he never ceases to laud. His little book was made short and easy to read, so as not to frighten, by a too arduous text, the readers whom he hoped to convince. He constantly gives the example of the " Ancients" to his contemporaries. The result is a sort of perfume of actuality, which had much to do with his success. It still is interesting reading and still is the subject of modern commentaries. No less than forty have appeared in Germany in the 19th and 20th centuries. Revue Mititare Generate (France) and our own Infantry Journal carried articles on Vegetius in 1938. Dankfried Schenk published an interesting article in Klio in 1930, which gives Vegetius the highest place among the writers of his time.

The present edition includes the first three books of Vegetius' work, omitting only repetitions. The fourth and fifth books, both very brief, deal with the attack and defense of fortified places and with naval operations. These are of interest only to military antiquarians and for that reason have not been included. The present translation was made by Lieutenant John Clarke and published in London in 1767. It is the best available in English and has been edited only to the minimum extent necessary to conform to modern usage.

An excellent discussion of Vegetius can be found in Warfare, by Spaulding, Nickerson and Wright, page 294, et sequens, Harcourt Brace & Co., 1925. Delpech, La Tactique au 13me Siecte, Paris, 1886, gives the best account of the influence of Vegetius on European military thought. Hans Delbruck's discussion of Vegetius in Geschichte der Kriegskunft, Vol. II, Berlin, 1921, although brief, is very acute.

Preface to Book I

To the Emperor Valentinian

It has been an old custom for authors to offer to their Princes the fruits of their studies in belles letters, from a persuasion that no work can be published with propriety but under the auspices of the Emperor, and that the knowledge of a Prince should be more general, and of the most important kind, as its influence is felt so keenly by all his subjects. We have many instances of the favorable reception which Augustus and his illustrious successors conferred on the works presented to them; and this encouragement of the Sovereign made the sciences flourish. The consideration of Your Majesty's superior indulgence for attempts of this sort, induced me to follow this example, and makes me at the same time almost forget my own inability when compared with the ancient writers. One advantage, however, I derive from the nature of this work, as it requires no elegance of expression, or extraordinary share of genius, but only great care and fidelity in collecting and explaining, for public use, the instructions and observations of our old historians of military affairs, or those who wrote expressly concerning them.

My design in this treatise is to exhibit in some order the peculiar customs and usages of the ancients in the choice and discipline of their new levies. Nor do I presume to offer this work.to Your Majesty from a supposition that you are not acquainted with every part of its contents; but that you may see that the same salutary dispositions and regulations which your own wisdom prompts You to establish for the happiness of the Empire, were formerly observed by the founders thereof; and that Your Majesty may find with ease in this abridgement whatever is most useful on so necessary and important a subject.

De Re Militari Book I: The Selection and Training of New Levies

THE ROMAN DISCIPLINE - THE CAUSE OF THEIR GREATNESS

Victory in war does not depend entirely upon numbers or mere courage; only skill and discipline will insure it. We find that the Romans owed the conquest of the world to no other cause than continual military training, exact observance of discipline in their camps and unwearied cultivation of the other arts of war. Without these, what chance would the inconsiderable numbers of the Roman armies have had against the multitudes of the Gauls? Or with what success would their small size have been opposed to the prodigious stature of the Germans? The Spaniards surpassed us not only in numbers, but in physical strength. We were always inferior to the Africans in wealth and unequal to them in deception and stratagem. And the Greeks, indisputably, were far superior to us in skill in arts and all kinds of knowledge.

But to all these advantages the Romans opposed unusual care in the choice of their levies and in their military training. They thoroughly understood the importance of hardening them by continual practice, and of training them to every maneuver that might happen in the line and in action. Nor were they less strict in punishing idleness and sloth. The courage of a soldier is heightened by his knowledge of his profession, and he only wants an opportunity to execute what he is convinced he has been perfectly taught. A handful of men, inured to war, proceed to certain victory, while on the contrary numerous armies of raw and undisciplined troops are but multitudes of men dragged to slaughter.

THE SELECTION OF RECRUITS

To treat our subject with some method, we shall first examine what provinces or nations are to be preferred for supplying the armies with recruits. It is certain that every country produces both brave men and cowards; but it is equally as certain that some nations are naturally more warlike than others, and that courage, as well as strength of body, depends greatly upon the influence of the different climates.

We shall next examine whether the city or the country produces the best and most capable soldiers. No one, I imagine, can doubt that the peasants are the most fit to carry arms for they from their infancy have been exposed to all kinds of weather and have been brought up to the hardest labor. They are able to endure the greatest heat of the sun, are unacquainted with the use of baths, and are strangers to the other luxuries of life. They are simple, content with little, inured to all kinds of fatigue, and prepared in some measure for a military life by their continual employment in their country-work, in handling the spade, digging trenches and carrying burdens. In cases of necessity, however, they are sometimes obliged to make levies in the cities. And these men, as soon as enlisted, should be taught to work on entrenchments, to march in ranks, to carry heavy burdens, and to bear the sun and dust. Their meals should be coarse and moderate; they should be accustomed to lie sometimes in the open air and sometimes in tents. After this, they should be instructed in the use of their arms. And if any long expedition is planned, they should be encamped as far as possible from the temptations of the city. By these precautions their minds, as well as their bodies, will properly be prepared for the service.

I realize that in the first ages of the Republic, the Romans always raised their armies in the city itself, but this was at a time when there were no pleasures, no luxuries to enervate them. The Tiber was then their only bath, and in it they refreshed themselves after their exercises and fatigues in the field by swimming. In those days the same man was both soldier and farmer, but a farmer who, when occasion arose, laid aside his tools and put on the sword. The truth of this is confirmed by the instance of Quintius Cincinnatus, who was following the plow when they came to offer him the dictatorship. The chief strength of our armies, then, should be recruited from the country. For it is certain that the less a man is acquainted with the sweets of life, the less reason he has to be afraid of death.

THE PROPER AGE FOR RECRUITS

If we follow the ancient practice, the proper time for enlisting youth into the army is at their entrance into the age of puberty. At this time instructions of every kind are more quickly imbibed and more lastingly imprinted on the mind. Besides this, the indispensable military exercises of running and leaping must be acquired before the limbs are too much stiffened by age. For it is activity, improved by continual practice, which forms the useful and good soldier. Formerly, says Sallust, the Roman youth, as soon as they were of an age to carry arms, were trained in the Strictest manner in their camps to all the fatigues and exercises of war. For it is certainly better that a soldier, perfectly disciplined, should, through emulation, repine at his not being yet arrived at a proper age for action, than have the mortification of knowing it is past. A sufficient time is also required for his instruction in the different branches of the service. It is no easy matter to train the horse or foot archer, or to form the legionary soldier to every part of the drill, to teach him not to quit his post, to keep ranks, to take a proper aim and throw his missile weapons with force, to dig trenches, to plant palisades, how to manage his shield, glance off the blows of the enemy, and how to parry a stroke with dexterity. A soldier, thus perfect in his business, so far from showing any backwardness to engage, will be eager for an opportunity of signaling himself.

THEIR SIZE

We find the ancients very fond of procuring the tallest men they could for the service, since the standard for the cavalry of the wings and for the infantry of the first legionary cohorts was fixed at six feet, or at least five feet ten inches. These requirements might easily be kept up in those times when such numbers followed the profession of arms and before it was the fashion for the flower of Roman youth to devote themselves to the civil offices of state. But when necessity requires it, the height of a man is not to be regarded so much as his strength; and for this we have the authority of Homer, who tells us that the deficiency of stature in Tydeus was amply compensated by his vigor and courage.

SIGNS OF DESIRABLE QUALITIES

Those employed to superintend new levies should be particularly careful in examining the features of their faces, their eyes, and the make of their limbs, to enable them to form a true judgment and choose such as are most likely to prove good soldiers. For experience assures us that there are in men, as well as in horses and dogs, certain signs by which their virtues may be discovered. The young soldier, therefore, ought to have a lively eye, should carry his head erect, his chest should be broad, his shoulders muscular and brawny, his fingers long, his arms strong, his waist small, his shape easy, his legs and feet rather nervous than fleshy. When all these marks are found in a recruit, a little height may be dispensed with, since it is of much more importance that a soldier should be strong than tall.

TRADES PROPER FOR NEW LEVIES

In choosing recruits regard should be given to their trade. Fishermen, fowlers, confectioners, weavers, and in general all whose professions more properly belong to women should, in my opinion, by no means be admitted into the service. On the contrary, smiths, carpenters, butchers, and huntsmen are the most proper to be taken into it. On the careful choice of soldiers depends the welfare of the Republic, and the very essence of the Roman Empire and its power is so inseparably connected with this charge, that it is of the highest importance not to be intrusted indiscriminately, but only to persons whose fidelity can be relied on. The ancients considered Sertorius' care in this point as one of the most eminent of his military qualifications. The soldiery to whom the defense of the Empire is consigned and in whose hands is the fortune of war, should, if possible, be of reputable families and unexceptionable in their manners. Such sentiments as may be expected in these men will make good soldiers. A sense of honor, by preventing them from behaving ill, will make them victorious.

But what good can be expected from a man by nature a coward, though ever so well disciplined or though he has served ever so many campaigns? An army raised without proper regard to the choice of its recruits was never yet made good by length of time; and we are now convinced by fatal experience that this is the source of all our misfortunes. So many defeats can only be imputed to the effects of a long peace which has made us negligent and careless in the choice of our levies and to the inclination so prevalent among the better sort in preferring the civil posts of the government to the profession of arms and to the shameful conduct of the superintendents, who, through interest or connivance, accept many men which those who are obliged to furnish substitutes for the army choose to send, and admit such men into the service as the masters themselves would not even keep for servants. Thus it appears that a trust of such importance should be committed to none but men of merit and integrity.

THE MILITARY MARK

The recruit, however, should not receive the military mark* as soon as enlisted. He must first be tried if fit for service; whether he has sufficient activity and strength; if he has capacity to learn his duty; and whether he has the proper degree of military courage. For many, though promising enough in appearance, are found very unfit upon trial. These are to be rejected and replaced by better men; for it is not numbers, but bravery which carries the day.

After their examination, the recruits should then receive the military mark, and be taught the use of their arms by constant and daily exercise. But this essential custom has been abolished by the relaxation introduced by a long peace. We cannot now expect to find a man to teach what he never learned himself. The only method, therefore, that remains of recovering the ancient customs is by books, and by consulting the old historians. But they are of little service to us in this respect, as they only relate the exploits and events of wars, and take no notice of the objects of our present enquiries, which they considered as universally known.

INITIAL TRAINING

The first thing the soldiers are to be taught is the military step, which can only be acquired by constant practice of marching quick and together. Nor is anything of more consequence either on the march or in the line than that they should keep their ranks with the greatest exactness. For troops who march in an irregular and disorderly manner are always in great danger of being defeated. They should march with the common military step twenty miles in five summer-hours, and with the full step, which is quicker, twenty-four miles in the same number of hours. If they exceed this pace, they no longer march but run, and no certain rate can be assigned.

But the young recruits in particular must be exercised in running, in order to charge the enemy with great vigor; occupy, on occasion, an advantageous post with greater expedition, and prevent the enemy in their designs upon the same; that they may, when sent to reconnoiter, advance with speed, return with greater celerity and more easily come up with the enemy in a pursuit.

Leaping is another very necessary exercise, to enable them to pass ditches or embarrassing eminences of any kind without trouble or difficulty. There is also another very material advantage to be derived from these exercises in time of action; for a soldier who advances with his javelin,.running and leaping, dazzles the eyes of his adversary, strikes him with terror, and gives him the fatal stroke before he has time to put himself on his defense. Sallust, speaking of the excellence of Pompey the Great in these particulars, tells us that he disputed the superiority in leaping with the most active, in running with the most swift, and in exercises of strength with the most robust. Nor would he ever have been able to have opposed Serrorius with success, if he had not prepared both himself and his soldiers for action by continual exercises of this sort.

TO LEARN TO SWIM

Every young soldier, without exception, should in the summer months be taught to swim; for it is sometimes impossible to pass rivers on bridges, but the flying and pursuing army both are often obliged to swim over them. A sudden melting of snow or fall of rain often makes them overflow their banks, and in such a situation, the danger is as great from ignorance in swimming as from the enemy. The ancient Romans, therefore, perfected in every branch of the military art by a continued series of wars and perils, chose the Field of Mars as the most commodious for their exercises on account of its vicinity to the Tiber, that the youth might therein wash off the sweat and dust, and refresh themselves after their fatigues by swimming. The cavalry also as well as the infantry, and even the horses and the servants of the army should be accustomed to this exercise, as they are all equally liable to the same accidents.

THE POST EXERCISE

We are informed by the writings of the ancients that, among their other exercises, they had that of the post. They gave their recruits round bucklers woven with willows, twice as heavy as those used on real service, and wooden swords double the weight of the common ones. They exercised them with these at the post both morning and afternoon.

This is an invention of the greatest use, not only to soldiers, but also to gladiators. No man of either profession ever distinguished himself in the circus or field of battle, who was not perfect in this kind of exercise. Every soldier, therefore, fixed a post firmly in the ground, about the height of six feet. Against this, as against a real enemy, the recruit was exercised with the above mentioned arms, as it were with the common shield and sword, sometimes aiming At the head or face, sometimes at the sides, at others endeavoring to strike at the thighs or legs. He was instructed in what manner to advance and retire, and in short how to take every advantage of his adversary; but was thus above all particularly cautioned not to lay himself open to his antagonist while aiming his stroke at him.

NOT TO CUT, BUT TO THRUST WITH THE SWORD

They were likewise taught not to cut but to thrust with their swords. For the Romans not only made a jest of those who fought with the edge of that weapon, but always found them an easy conquest. A stroke with the edges, though made with ever so much force, seldom kills, as the vital parts of the body are defended both by the bones and armor. On the contrary, a stab, though it penetrates but two inches, is generally fatal. Besides in the attitude of striking, it is impossible to avoid exposing the right arm and side; but on the other hand, the body is covered while a thrust is given, and the adversary receives the point before he sees the sword. This was the method of fighting principally used by the Romans, and their reason for exercising recruits with arms of such a weight at first was, that when they came to carry the common ones so much lighter, the greater difference might enable them to act with greater security and alacrity in time of action.

THE DRILL CALLED ARMATURA

The new levies also should be taught by the masters at arms the system of drill called armatura, as it is still partly kept up among us. Experience even at this time convinces us that soldiers, perfect therein, are of the most service in engagements. And they afford certain proofs of the importance and effects of discipline in the difference we see between those properly trained in this branch of drill and the other troops. The old Romans were so conscious of its usefulness that they rewarded the masters at arms with a double allowance of provision. The soldiers who were backward in this drill were punished by having their allowance in barley. Nor did they receive it as usual, in wheat, until they had, in the presence of the prefect, tribunes, or other principal officers of the legion, showed sufficient proofs of their knowledge of every part of their study.

No state can either be happy or secure that is remiss and negligent in the discipline of its troops. For it is not profusion of riches or excess of luxury that can influence our enemies to court or respect us. This can only be effected by the terror of our arms. It is an observation of Cato that. misconduct in the common affairs of life may be retrieved, but that it is quite otherwise in war, where errors are fatal and without remedy, and are followed by immediate punishment. For the consequences of engaging an enemy, without skill or courage, is that part of the army is left on the field of battle, and those who remain receive such an impression from their defeat that they dare not afterwards look the enemy in the face.

THE USE OF MISSILE WEAPONS

Besides the aforementioned exercise of the recruits at the post, they were furnished with javelins of greater weight than common, which they were taught to throw at the same post. And the masters at arms were very careful to instruct them how to cast them with a proper aim and force. This practice strengthens the arm and makes the soldier a good marksman.

THE USE OF THE BOW

A third or fourth of the youngest and fittest soldiers should also be exercised at the post with bows and arrows made for that purpose only. The masters for this branch must be chosen with care and must apply themselves diligently to teach the men to hold the bow in a proper position, to bend it with strength, to keep the left hand steady. to draw the right with skill, to direct both the attention and the eye to the object, and to take their aim with equal certainty either on foot or on horseback. But this is not to be acquired without great application, nor to be retained without daily exercise and practice.

The utility of good archers in action is evidently demonstrated by Cato in his treatise on military discipline. To the institution of a body of troops of this sort Claudius owed his victory over an enemy who, till that time, had constantly been superior to him. Scipio Africanus, before his battle with the Numantines, who had made a Roman army ignominiously pass under the yoke, thought he could have no likelihood of success except by mingling a number of select archers with every century.

THE SLING

Recruits are to be taught the art of throwing stones both with the hand and sling. The inhabitants of the Balearic Islands are said to have been the inventors of slings, and to have managed them with surprising dexterity, owing to the manner of bringing up their children. The children were not allowed to have their food by their mothers till they had first struck it with their sling. Soldiers, notwithstanding their defensive armor, are often more annoyed by the round stones from the sling than by all the arrows of the enemy. Stones kill without mangling the body, and the contusion is mortal without loss of blood. It is universally known the ancients employed slingers in all their engagements. There is the greater reason for instructing all troops, without exception, in this exercise, as the sling cannot be reckoned any incumbrance, and often is of the greatest service, especially when they are obliged to engage in stony places, to defend a mountain or an eminence, or to repulse an enemy at the attack of a castle or city.

THE LOADED JAVELIN

The exercise of the loaded javelins, called martiobarbuli, must not be omitted. We formerly had two legions in Illyricum, consisting of six thousand men each, which from their extraordinary dexterity and skill in the use of these weapons were discingui.shed by the same appellation. They supported for a long time the weight of all the wars and distinguished themselves so remarkably that the Emperors Diocletian and Maximian on their accession honored them with the titles of Jovian and Herculean and preferred them before all the other legions. Every soldier carries five of these javelins in the hollow of his shield. And thus the legionary soldiers seem to supply the place of archers, for they wound both the men and horses of the enemy before they come within reach of the common missile weapons.

TO BE TAUGHT TO VAULT

The ancients strictly obliged both the veteran soldiers and recruits to a constant practice of vaulting. It has indeed reached our cimes, although little regard is paid to it at present. They had wooden horses for that purpose placed in winter under cover and in summer in the field. The young soldiers were taught to vault on them at first without arms, afterwards completely armed. And such was their attention to this exercise that they were accustomed to mount and dismount on either side indifferently, with their drawn swords or lances in their hands. By assiduous practice in the leisure of peace, their cavalry was brought to such perfection of discipline that they mounted their horses in an instant even amidst the confusion of sudden and unexpected alarms.

AND TO CARRY BURDENS

To accustom soldiers to carry burdens is also an essential part of discipline. Recruits in particular should be obliged frequently to carry a weight of not less than sixty pounds (exclusive of their arms), and to march with it in the ranks. This is because on difficult expeditions they often find themselves under the necessity of carrying their provisions as well as their arms. Nor will they find this troublesome when inured to it by custom, which makes everything easy. Our troops in ancient times were a proof of this, and Virgil has remarked it in the following lines:

The Roman soldiers, bred in war's alarms,
Bending with unjust loads and heavy arms,
Cheerful their toilsome marches undergo,
And pitch their sudden camp before the foe.

THE ARMS OF THE ANCIENTS

The manner of arming the troops comes next under consideration. But the method of the ancients no longer is followed. For though after the example of the Goths, the Alans and the Huns, we have made some improvements in the arms of the cavalry, yet it is plain the infantry are entirely defenseless. From the foundation of the city till the reign of the Emperor Gratian, the foot wore cuirasses and helmets. But negligence and sloth having by degrees introduced a total relaxation of discipline, the soldiers began to think their armor too heavy, as they seldom put it on. They first requested leave from the Emperor to lay aside the cuirass and afterwards the helmet. In consequence of this, our troops in their engagements with the Goths were often overwhelmed with their showers of arrows. Nor was the necessity of obliging the infantry to resume their cuirasses and helmets discovered, notwithstanding such repeated defeats, which brought on the destruction of so many great cities.

Troops, defenseless and exposed to all the weapons of the enemy, are more disposed to fly than fight. What can be expected from a foot-archer without cuirass or helmet, who cannot hold at once his bow and shield; or from the ensigns whose bodies are naked, and who cannot at the same time carry a shield and the colors? The foot soldier finds the weight of a cuirass and even of a helmet intolerable. This is because he is so seldom exercised and rarely puts them on.

But the case would be quite different, were they even heavier than they are, if by constant practice he had been accustomed to wear them. But it seems these very men, who cannot support the weight of the ancient armor, think nothing of exposing themselves without defense to wounds and death, or, which is worse, to the shame of being made prisoners, or of betraying their country by flight; and thus to avoid an inconsiderable share of exercise and fatigue, suffer themselves ignominiously to be cut in pieces. With what propriety could the ancients call the infantry a wall, but that in some measure they resembled it by the complete armor of the legionary soldiers who had shields, helmets, cuirasses, and greaves of iron on the right leg; and the archers who had gauntlets on the left arm. These were the defensive arms of the legionary soldiers. Those who fought in the first line of their respective legions were called principes, in the second hastati, and in third triarii.

The triarii, according to their method of discipline, rested in time of action on one knee, under cover of their shields, so that in this position they might be less exposed to the darts of the enemy than if they stood upright; and also, when there was a necessity for bringing them up, that they might be fresh, in full vigor and charge with the greater impetuosity. There have been many instances of their gaining a complete victory after the entire defeat of both the principes and hastati.

The ancients had likewise a body of light infantry, slingers, and ferentarii (the light troops), who were generally posted on the wings and began the engagement. The most active and best disciplined men were selected for this service; and as their number was not very great, they easily retired in case of a repulse through the intervals of the legion, without thus occasioning the least disorder in the line.

The Pamonian leather caps worn by our soldiers were formerly introduced with a different design. The ancients obliged the men to wear them at all times so that being constantly accustomed to have the head covered they might be less sensible of the weight of the helmet.

As to the missile weapons of the infantry, they were javelins headed with a triangular sharp iron, eleven inches or a foot long, and were called piles. When once fixed in the shield it was impossible to draw them out, and when thrown with force and skill, they penetrated the cuirass without difficulty. At present they are seldom used by us, but are the principal weapon of the barbarian heavy-armed foot. They are called bebrae, and every man carries two or three of them to battle.

It must be observed that when the soldiers engage with the javelin, the left foot should be advanced, for, by this attitude the force required to throw it is considerably increased. On the contrary, when they are close enough to use their piles and swords, the right foot should be advanced, so that the body may present less aim to the enemy, and the right arm be nearer and in a more advantageous position for striking. Hence it appears that it is as necessary to provide soldiers with defensive arms of every kind as to instruct them in the use of offensive ones. For it is certain a man will fight with greater courage and confidence when he finds himself properly armed for defense.

ENTRENCHED CAMPS

Recruits are to be instructed in the manner of entrenching camps, there being no part of discipline so necessary and useful as this. For in a camp, well chosen and entrenched, the troops both day and night lie secure within their works, even though in view of the enemy. It seems to resemble a fortified city which they can build for their safety wherever they please. But this valuable art is now entirely lost, for it is long since any of our camps have been fortified either with trenches or palisades. By this neglect our forces have been often surprised by day and night by the enemy's cavalry and suffered very severe losses. The importance of this custom appears not only from the danger to which troops are perpetually exposed who encamp without such precautions, but from the distressful situation of an army that, after receiving a check in the field, finds itself without retreat and consequently at the mercy of the enemy. A camp, especially in the neighborhood of an enemy, must be chosen with great care. Its situation should be strong by nature, and there should be plenty of wood, forage and water. If the army is to continue in it any considerable time, attention must be had to the salubrity of the place. The camp must not be commanded by any higher grounds from whence it might be insulted or annoyed by the enemy, nor must the location be liable to floods which would expose the army to great danger. The dimensions of the camps must be determined by the number of troops and quantity of baggage, that a large army may have room enough, and that a small one may not be obliged to extend itself beyond its proper ground. The form of the camps must be determined by the site of the country, in conformity to which they must be square, triangular or oval. The Praetorian gate should either front the east or the enemy. In a temporary camp it should face the route by which the army is to march. Within this gate the tents of the first centuries or cohorts are pitched, and the dragons* and other ensigns planted.

The Decumane gate is directly opposite to the Praetorian in the rear of the camp, and through this the soldiers are conducted to the place appointed for punishment or execution.

There are two methods of entrenching a camp. When the danger is not imminent, they carry a slight ditch round the whole circuit, only nine feet broad and seven deep. With the turf taken from this they make a kind of wall or breastwork three feet high on the inner side of the ditch. But where there is reason to be apprehensive of attempts of the enemy, the camp must be surrounded with a regular ditch twelve feet broad and nine feet deep perpendicular from the surface of the ground. A parapet is then raised on the side next the camp, of the height of four feet, with hurdles and fascines properly covered and secured by the earth taken out of the ditch. From these dimensions the interior height of the intrenchment will be found to be thirteen feet, and the breadth of the ditch twelve. On the top of the whole are planted strong palisades which the soldiers carry constantly with them for this purpose. A sufficient number of spades, pickaxes, wicker baskets and tools of all kinds are to be provided for these works.

There is no difficulty in carrying on the fortifications of a camp when no enemy is in sight. But if the enemy is near, all the cavalry and half the infantry are to be drawn up in order of battle to cover the rest of the troops at work on the entrenchments and be ready to receive the enemy if they offer to attack. The centuries are employed by turns on the work and are regularly called to the relief by a crier till the whole is completed. It is then inspected and measured by the centurions, who punish such as have been indolent or negligent. This is a very important point in the discipline of young soldiers, who when properly trained to it will be able in an emergency to fortify their camp with skill and expedition.

EVOLUTIONS

No part of drill is more essential in action than for soldiers to keep their ranks with the greatest exactness, without opening or closing too much. Troops too much crowded can never fight as they ought, and only embarrass one another. If their order is too open and loose, they give the enemy an opportunity of penetrating. Whenever this happens and they are attacked in the rear, universal disorder and confusion are inevitable. Recruits should therefore be constantly in the field, drawn up by the roll and formed at first into a single rank. They should learn to dress in a straight line and to keep an equal and just distance between man and man. They must then be ordered to double the rank, which they must perform very quickly, and instantly cover their file leaders. In the next place, they are to double again and form four deep. And then the triangle or, as it is commonly called, the wedge, a disposition found very serviceable in action. They must be taught to form the circle or orb; for well-disciplined troops, after being broken by the enemy, have thrown themselves into this position and have thereby prevented the total rout of the army. These evolutions, often practiced in the field of exercise, will be found easy in execution on actual service.

MONTHLY MARCHES

It was a constant custom among the old Romans, confirmed by the Ordinances of Augustus and Hadrian, to exercise both cavalry and infantry three times in a month by marches of a certain length. The foot were obliged to march completely armed the distance of ten miles from the camp and return, in the most exact order and with the military step which they changed and quickened on some part of the march. Their cavalry likewise, in troops and properly armed, performed the same marches and were exercised at the same time in their peculiar movement and evolutions; sometimes, as if pursuing the enemy, sometimes retreating and returning again with greater impetuosity to the charge. They made these marches not in plain and even ground only, but both cavalry and infantry were ordered into difficult and uneven places and to ascend or descend mountains, to prepare them for all kinds of accidents and familiarize them with the different maneuvers that the various situations of a country may require.

CONCLUSION

These military maxims and instructions, invincible Emperor, as a proof of my devotion and zeal for your service, I have carefully collected from the works of all the ancient authors on the subject. My design herein is to point out the certain method of forming good and serviceable armies, which can only be accomplished by an exact imitation of the ancients in their care in the choice and discipline of their levies. Men are not degenerated in point of courage, nor are the countries that produced the Lacedaemonians, the Athenians, the Marsians, the Samnites, the Peligni and even the Romans themselves, yet exhausted. Did not the Epirots acquire in former times a great reputation in war? Did not the Macedonians and Thessalians, after conquering the Persians, penetrate even into India? And it is well known that the warlike dispositions of the Dacians, Moesians and Thracians gave rise to the fable that Mars was born among them.

To pretend to enumerate the different nations so formidable of old, all which now are subject to the Romans, would be tedious. But the security established by long peace has altered their dispositions, drawn them off from military to civil pursuits and infused into them a love of idleness and ease. Hence a relaxation of military discipline insensibly ensued, then a neglect of it, and it sunk at last into entire oblivion. Now will it appear surprising that this alteration should have happened in latter times, if we consider that the peace, which lasted about twenty years or somewhat more after the first Punic war, enervated the Romans, before everywhere victorious, by idleness and neglect of discipline to such a degree, that in the second Punic war they were not able to keep the field against Hannibal. At last, after the defeat of many consuls and the loss of many officers and armies, they were convinced that the revival of discipline was the only road to victory and thereby recovered their superiority. The necessity, therefore, of discipline cannot be too often inculcated, as well as the strict attention requisite in the choice and training of new levies. It is also certain that it is a much less expense to a State to train its own subjects to arms than to take foreigners into its pay.

* This mark was imprinted on the hands of the soldiers, either with a hot iron, or in some other manner. It was indelible.

* The dragon was the particular ensign of each cohort.

Preface to Book II

To the Emperor Valentinian

Such a continued series of victories and triumphs proved incontestably Your Majesty's full and perfect knowledge of the military discipline of the ancients. Success in any profession is the most certain mark of skill in it. By a greatness of mind. above human comprehension Your Majesty condescends to seek instruction from the ancients, notwithstanding your own recent exploits surpass antiquity itself. On receiving Your Majesty's orders to continue this abridgement, not so much for your instruction as convenience, I knew not how to reconcile my devotion to Your commands with the respect due to Your Majesty. Would it not be the greatest height of presumption to pretend to mention the art of war to the Lord and Master of the world and the Conqueror of all the barbarous nations, unless it were to describe his own actions? But disobedience to the will of so great a Prince would be both highly criminal and dangerous. My obedience, therefore, made me presumptuous, from the apprehensions of appearing more so by a contrary conduct. And in this I was not a little encouraged by the late instance of Your Majesty's indulgence. My treatise on the choice and discipline of new levies met with a favorable reception from Your Majesty, and since a work succeeded so well, composed of my own accord, I can have no fears for one undertaken by your own express commands.

Book II: The Organization of the Legion

THE MILITARY ESTABLISHMENT

The military establishment consists of three parts, the cavalry, infantry and marine. The wings of cavalry were so called from their similitude to wings in their extension on both sides of the main body for its protection. They are now called vexillations from the kind of standards peculiar to them. The legionary horse are bodies particularly annexed to each legion, and of a different kind; and on their model were organized the cavalry called Ocreati, from the light boots they wear. The fleet consists of two divisions, the one of men of war called Liburnae, and the other of armed sloops. The cavalry are designed for plains. Fleets are employed for the protection of seas and rivers. The infantry are proper for the defense of eminences, for the garrisons of cities and are equally serviceable in plain and in uneven ground. The latter, therefore, from their facility of acting everywhere, are certainly the most useful and necessary troops to a state exclusively of the consideration of their being maintained at a less expense. The infantry are divided into two corps, the legions and auxiliaries, the latter of which are furnished by allies or confederates. The peculiar strength of the Romans always consisted in the excellent organization of their legions. They were so denominated ab eligendo, from the care and exactness used in the choice of the soldiers. The number of legionary troops in an army is generally much more considerable than that of the auxiliaries.

DIFFERENCE BETWEEN THE LEGIONS AND AUXILIARIES

The Macedonians, the Greeks and the Dardanians formed their troops into phalanxes of eight thousand men each. The Gauls, Celtiberians and many other barbarous nations divided their armies into bodies of six thousand each. The Romans have their legions usually six thousand strong, sometImes more.

We shall now explain the difference between the legions and the auxiliaries. The latter are hired corps of foreigners assembled from different parts of the Empire, made up of different numbers, without knowledge of one another or any tie of affection. Each nation has its own peculiar discipline, customs and manner of fighting. Little can be expected from forces so dissimilar in every respect, since it is one of the most essential points in military undertakings that the whole army should be put in motion and governed by one and the same order. But it is almost impossible for men to act in concert under such varying and unsettled circumstances. They are, however, when properly trained and disciplined, of material service and are always joined as light troops with the legions in the line. And though the legions do not place their principal dependence on them, yet they look on them as a very considerable addition to their strength.

But the complete Roman legion, in its own peculiar cohorts, contains within itself the heavy-armed foot, that is: the principes, hastati, triarii, and antefignani, the light-armed foot, consisting of the ferentarii, archers, slingers, and balistarii, together with the legionary cavalry incorporated with it. These bodies, all actuated with the same spirit, are united inseparably in their various dispositions for forming, encamping and fighting. Thus the legion is compact and perfect in all its parts and, without any foreign assistance, has always been superior to any force that could be brought against it. The Roman greatness is a proof of the excellence of their legions, for with them they always defeated whatever numbers of the enemy they thought fit, or their circumstances gave them an opportunity to engage.

CAUSES OF DECAY OF THE LEGION

The name of the legion remains indeed to this day in our armies, but its strength and substance are gone, since by the neglect of our predecessors, honors and preferments, which were formerly the recompenses of merit and long services, were to be attained only by interest and favor. Care is no longer taken to replace the soldiers, who after serving their full time, have received their discharges. The vacancies continually happening by sickness, discharges, desertion and various other casualties, if not supplied every year or even every month, must in time disable the most numerous army. Another cause of the weakness of our legions is that in them the soldiers find the duty hard, the arms heavy, the rewards distant and the discipline severe. To avoid these inconveniences, the young men enlist in the auxiliaries, where the service is less laborious and they have reason to expect more speedy recompenses.

Cato the Elder, who was often Consul and always victorious at the head of the armies, believed he should do his country more essential service by writing on military affairs, than by all his exploits in the field. For the consequences of brave actions are only temporary, while whatever is committed to writing for public good is of lasting benefit. Several others have followed his example, particularly Frontinus, whose elaborate works on this subject were so well received by the Emperor Trajan. These are the authors whose maxims and institutions I have undertaken to abridge in the most faithful and conclse manner.

The expense of keeping up good or bad troops is the same; but it depends wholly on You, most August Emperor, to recover the excellent discipline of the ancients and to correct the abuses of later times. This is a reformation the advantages of which will be equally felt by ourselves and our posterity.

THE ORGANIZATION OF THE LEGION

All our writers agree that never more than two legions, besides auxiliaries, were sent under the command of each consul against the most numerous armies of the enemies. Such was the dependence on their discipline and resolution that this number was thought sufficient for any war they were engaged in. I shall therefore explain the organization of the ancient legion according to the military constitution. But if the description appear obscure or imperfect, it is not to be imputed to me, but to the difficulty of the subject itself, which is therefore to be examined with the greater attention. A prince, skilled himself in military affairs, has it in his power to make himself invincible by keeping up whatever number of well disciplined forces he thinks proper.

The recruits having thus been carefully chosen with proper attention to their persons and dispositions, and having been daily exercised for the space of four months at least, the legion is formed by the command and under the auspices of the Emperor. The military mark, which is indelible, is first imprinted on the hands of the new levies, and as their names are inserted in the roll of the legions they take the usual oath, called the military oath. They swear by God, by Christ and by the Holy Ghost; and by the Majesty of the Emperor who, after God, should be the chief object of the love and veneration of mankind. For when he has once received the title of August, his subjects are bound to pay him the most sincere devotion and homage, as the representative of God on earth. And every man, whether in a private or military station, serves God in serving him faithfully who reigns by His authority. The soldiers, therefore, swear they will obey the Emperor willingly and implicitly in all his commands, that they will never desert and will always be ready to sacrifice their lives for the Roman Empire.

The legion should consist of ten cohorts, the first of which exceeds the others both in number and quality of its soldiers, who are selected to serve in it as men of some family and education. This cohort has the care of the eagle, the chief ensign in the Roman armies and the standard of the whole legion, as well as of the images of the emperors which are always considered as sacred. It consists of eleven hundred and five foot and one hundred and thirty-two horse cuirassiers, and is distinguished by the name of the Millarian Cohort. It is the head of the legion and is always first formed on the right of the first line when the legion draws up in order of battle.

The second cohort contains five hundred and fifty-five foot and sixty-six horse, and is called the Quingentarian Cohort. The third is composed of five hundred and fiftyfive foot and sixty-six horse, generally chosen men, on account of its situation in the center of the first line. The fourth consists of the same number of five hundred and fifty-five foot and sixty-six horse. The fifth has likewise five hundred and fifty-five foot and sixty-six horse, which should be some of the best men, being posted on the left flank as the first cohort is on the right. These five cohorts compose the first line.

The sixth includes five hundred and fifty-five foot and sixty-six horse, which should be the flower of the young soldiers as it draws up in the rear of the eagle and the images of the emperors, and on the right of the second line. The seventh contains five hundred and fifty-five foot and sixty-six horse. The eighth is composed of five hundred and fifty-five foot and sixty-six horse, all selected troops, as it occupies the center of the second line. The ninth has five hundred and fifty-five foot and sixty-six horse. The tenth consists of the same number of five hundred and fifty-five foot and sixty-six horse and requires good men, as it closes the left flank of the second line. These ten cohorts form the complete legions, consisting in the whole of six thousand one hundred foot and seven hundred and twenty-six horses. A legion should never be composed of a less number of men, but it is sometimes stronger by the addition of other Millarian Cohorts.

THE OFFICERS OF THE LEGION

Having shown the ancient establishment of the legion, we shall now explain the names of the principal soldiers or, to use the proper term, the officers, and their ranks according to the present rolls of the legions. The first tribune is appointed by the express commission and choice of the Emperor. The second tribune rises to that rank by length of service. The tribunes are so called from their command over the soldiers, who were at first levied by Romulus out of the different tribes. The officers who in action commanded the orders or divisions are called Ordinarii. The Augustales were added by Augustus to the Ordinarii; and the Flaviales were appointed by Flavius Vespasian to double the number of the Augustales. The eagle-bearers and the image-bearers are those who carry the eagles and images of the Emperors. The Optiones are subaltern officers, so denominated from their being selected by the option of their superior officers, to do their duty as their substitutes or lieutenants in case of sickness or other accident. The ensign-bearers carry the ensigns and are called Draconarii. The Tesserarii deliver the parole and the orders of the general to the different messes of the soldiers. The Campignei or Antefignani are those whose duty it is to keep the proper exercises and discipline among the troops. The Metatores are ordered before the army to fix on the ground for its encampments. The Beneficiarii are so named from their owing their promotion to the benefit or interest of the Tribunes. The Librarii keep the legionary accounts. The Tubicines, Cornicines, and Buccinatores derive their appellations from blowing the trumpet, cornet, and buccina. Those who, expert in their exercises, receive a double allowance of provisions, are called Armaturae Duplares, and those who have but a single portion, Simplares. The Mensores mark out the ground by measure for the tents in an encampment, and assign the troops their respective quarters in garrison. The Torquati, so denominated from the gold collars given them in reward for their bravery, had besides this honor different allowances. Those who received double were called Torquati Duplares, and those who had only single, Simplares.

There were, for the same reason, Candidatii Duplares, and Candidatii Simplares. These are the principal soldiers or officers distinguished by their rank and privileges thereto annexed. The rest are called Munifices, or working soldiers, from their being obliged to every kind of military work without exception. Formerly it was the rule that the first Princeps of the legion should be promoted regularly to the rank of Centurion of the Primiple. He not only was entrusted with the eagle but commanded four centuries, that is, four hundred men in the first line. As head of the legion he had appointments of great honor and profit. The first Hastatus had the command of two centuries or two hundred men in the second line, and is now called Ducenarius. The Princeps of the first cohort commanded a century and a half, that is, one hundred and fifty men, and kept in a great measure the general detail of the legion. The second Hastatus had likewise a century and a half, or one hundred and fifty men. The first Triarius had the command of one hundred men. Thus the ten centuries of the first cohort were commanded by five Ordinarii, who by the ancient establishment enjoyed great honors and emoluments that were annexed to this rank in order to inspire the soldiers of the legions with emulation to attain such ample and considerable rewards. They had also Centurions appointed to each century, now called Centenarii and Decani, who commanded ten men, now called heads of messes. The second cohort had five Centurions; and all the rest to the tenth inclusively the same number. In the whole legion there were fiftyfive.

Lieutenants of consular dignity were formerly sent to command in the armies under the general, and their authority extended over both the legions and auxiliaries in peace and war. Instead of these officers, persons of high rank are now substituted with the title of Masters of the Forces. They are not limited to the command of two legions only, but have often a greater number. But the peculiar officer of the legion was the Praefect, who was always a count of the first order. On him the chief command devolved in the absence of the lieutenant. The Tribunes, Centurions, and all the soldiers in general were under his orders: He gave out the parole and order for the march and for the guards. And if a soldier committed a crime, by his authority the Tribune adjudged him to punishment. He had charge of the arms, horses, clothing and provisions. It was also his duty to keep both the legionary horse and foot in daily exercise and to maintain the strictest discipline. He ought to be a careful and diligent officer, as the sole charge of forming the legion to regularity and obedience depended on him and the excellence of the soldiers redounded entirely to his own honor and credit.

The Praefect of the camp, though inferior in rank to the former, had a post of no small importance. The position of the camp, the direction of the entrenchments, the inspection of the tents or huts of the soldiers and the baggage were comprehended in his province. His authority extended over the sick, and the physicians who had the care of them; and he regulated the expenses relative thereto. He had the charge of providing carriages, bathorses and the proper tools for sawing and cutting wood, digging trenches, raising parapets, sinking wells and bringing water into the camp. He likewise had the care of furnishing the troops with wood and straw, as well as the rams, onagri, balistae and all the other engines of war under his direction. This post was always conferred on an officer of great skill, experience and long service, and who consequently was capable of instructing others in those branches of the profession in which he had distinguished himself.

THE PRAEFECT OF THE WORKMEN

The legion had a train of joiners, masons, carpenters, smiths, painters, and workmen of every kind for the construction of barracks in the winter-camps and for making or repairing the wooden towers, arms, carriages and the various sorts of machines and engines for the attack or defense of places. They had also traveling workshops in which they made shields, cuirasses, helmets, bows, arrows, javelins and offensive and defensive arms of all kinds. The ancients made it their chief care to have every thing for the service of the army within the camp. They even had a body of miners who, by working under ground and piercing the foundations of walls, according to the practice of the Beffi, penetrated into the body of a place. All these were under the direction of the officer called the praefect of the workmen.

THE TRIBUNE OF THE SOLDIERS

We have observed that the legions had ten cohorts, the first of which, called the Millarian Cohort, was composed of men selected on account of their circumstances, birth, education, person and bravery. The tribune who commanded them was likewise distinguished for his skill in his exercises, for the advantages of his person and the integrity of his manners. The other cohorts were commanded, according to the Emperor's pleasure, either by tribunes or other officers commissioned for that purpose. In former times the discipline was so strict that the tribunes or officers abovementioned not only caused the troops under their command to be exercised daily in their presence, but were themselves so perfect in their military exercises as to set them the example. Nothing does so much honor to the abilities or application of the tribune as the appearance and discipline of the soldiers, when their apparel is neat and clean, their arms bright and in good order and when they perform their exercises and evolutions with dexterity.

CENTURIES AND ENSIGNS OF THE FOOT

The chief ensign of the whole legion is the eagle and is carried by the eagle-bearer. Each cohort has also its own peculiar ensign, the Dragon, carried by the Draconarius. The ancients, knowing the ranks were easily disordered in the confusion of action, divided the cohorts into centuries and gave each century an ensign inscribed with the number both of the cohort and century so that the men keeping it in sight might be prevented from separating from their comrades in the greatest tumults. Besides the centurions, now called centenarii, were distinguished by different crests on their helmets, to be more easily known by the soldiers of their respective centuries. These precautions prevented any mistake, as every century was guided not only by its own ensign but likewise by the peculiar form of the helmet of its commanding officers. The centuries were also subdivided into messes of ten men each who lay in the same tent and were under orders and inspection of a Decanus or head of the mess. These messes were also called Maniples from their constant custom of fighting together in the same company or division.

LEGIONARY TROOPS OF HORSE

As the divisions of the infantry are called centuries, so those of the cavalry are called troops. A troop consists of thirty-two men and is commanded by a Decurion. Every century has its ensign and every troop its Standard. The centurion in the infantry is chosen for his size, strength and deXterity in throwing his missile weapons and for his skill in the use of his sword and shield; in short for his expertness in all the exercises. He is to be vigilant, temperate, accive and readier to execute the orders he receives than to talk; Strict in exercising and keeping up proper discipline among his soldiers, in obliging them to appear clean and well-dressed and to have their arms constantly rubbed and bright. In like manner the Decurion is to be preferred to the command of a troop for his activity and address in mounting his horse completely armed; for his skill in riding and in the use of the lance and bow; for his attencion in forming his men to all the evolutions of the cavalry; and for his care in obliging them to keep their cuirasses, lances and helmets always bright and in good order. The splendor of the arms has no inconsiderable effect in striking terror into an enemy. Can that man be reckoned a good soldier who through negligence suffers his arms to be spoiled by dirt and rust? In short, it is the duty of the Decurion to be attentive to whatever concerns the health or discipline of the men or horses in his troop.

DRAWING UP A LEGION IN ORDER OF BATTLE

We shall exemplify the manner of drawing up an army in order of battle in the instance of one legion, which may serve for any number. The cavalry are posted on the wings. The infantry begin to form on a line with the :first cohort on the right. The second cohort draws up on the left of the first; the third occupies the center; the fourth is posted next; and the fifth closes the left flank. The ordinarii, the other officers and the soldiers of the first line, ranged before and round the ensigns, were called the principes. They were all heavy armed troops and had helmets, cuirasses, greaves, and shields. Their offensive weapons were large swords, called spathae, and smaller ones called semispathae together with five loaded javelins in the concavity of the shield, which they threw at the first charge. They had likewise two other javelins, the largest of which was composed of a staff five feet and a half long and a triangular head of iron nine inches long. This was formerly called the pilum, but now it is known by the name of spiculum. The soldiers were particularly exercised in the use of this weapon, because when thrown with force and skill it often penetrated the shields of the foot and the cuirasses of the horse. The other javelin was of smaller size; its triangular point was only five inches long and the staff three feet and one half. It was anciently called verriculum but now verutum.

The first line, as I said before, was composed of the principes; the hastati formed the second and were armed in the same manner. In the second line the sixth cohort was posted on the right flank, with the seventh on its left; the eighth drew up in the center; the ninth was the next; and the tenth always closed the left flank. In the rear of these two lines were the ferentarii, light infantry and the troops armed with shields, loaded javelins, swords and common missile weapons, much in the same manner as our modern soldiers. This was also the post of the archers who had helmets, cuirasses, swords, bows and arrows; of the slingers who threw stones with the common sling or with the fustibalus; and of the tragularii who annoyed the enemy with arrows from the manubalistae or arcubalistae.

In the rear of all the lines, the triarii, completely armed, were drawn up. They had shields, cuirasses, helmets, greaves, swords, daggers, loaded javelins, and two of the common missile weapons. They rested during the acnon on one knee, so that if the first lines were obliged to give way, they might be fresh when brought up to the charge, and thereby retrieve what was lost and recover the victory. All the ensigns though, of the infantry, wore cuirasses of a smaller sort and covered their helmets with the shaggy skins of beasts to make themselves appear more terrible to the enemy. But the centurions had complete cuirasses, shields, and helmets of iron, the crest of which, placed transversely thereon, were ornamented with silver that they might be more easily distinguished by their respective soldiers.

The following disposition deserves the greatest attention. In the beginning of an engagement, the first and second lines remained immovable on their ground, and the trairii in their usual positions. The light-armed

troops, composed as above mentioned, advanced in the front of the line, and attacked the enemy. If they could make them give way, they pursued them; but if they were repulsed by superior bravery or numbers, they retired behind their own heavy armed infantry, which appeared like a wall of iron and renewed the action, at first with their missile weapons, then sword in hand. If they broke the enemy they never pursued them, least they should break their ranks or throw the line into confusion, and lest the enemy, taking advantage of their disorder, should return to the attack and destroy them without difficulty. The pursuit therefore was entirely left to the light-armed troops and the cavalry. By these precautions and dispositions the legion was victorious without danger, or if the contrary happened, was preserved without any considerable loss, for as it is not calculated for pursuit, it is likewise not easily thrown into disorder.

NAMES OF SOLDIERS INSCRIBED ON THEIR SHIELDS

Lest the soldiers in the confusion of battle should be separated from their comrades, every cohort had its shields painted in a manner peculiar to itself. The name of each soldier was also written on his shield, together with the number of the cohort and century to which he belonged. From this description we may compare the legion, when in proper order, to a well fortified city as containing within itself every thing requisite in war, wherever it moved. It was secure from any sudden attempt or surprise of an enemy by its expeditious method of entrenching its camp even in the open plains and it was always provided with troops and arms of every kind. To be victorious, therefore, over our enemies in the field, we must unanimously supplicate heaven to dispose the Emperor to reform the abuses in raising our levies and to recruit our legions after the method of the ancients. The same care in choosing and instructing our young soldiers in all military exercises and drills will soon make them equal to the old Roman troops who subdued the whole world. Nor let this alteration and loss of ancient discipline in any way affect Your Majesty, since it is a happiness reserved for You alone both to restore the ancient ordinances and establish new ones for the public welfare. Every work before the attempt carries in it an appearance of difficulty; but in this case, if the levies are made by careful and experienced officers, an army may be raised, disciplined and rendered fit for service in a very short time; for the necessary expenses once provided, diligence soon effects whatever it undertakes.

RECORDS AND ACCOUNTS

Several posts in the legion requiring men of some education, the superintendents of the levies should select some recruits for their skill in writing and accounts, besides the qualification to be attended to in general, such as size, strength and proper disposition for the service. For the whole detail of the legion, including the lists of the soldiers exempted from duty on private accounts, the rosters for their tour of military duties and their pay lists, is daily entered in the legionary books and kept we may almost say, with greater exactness than the regulations of provisions or other civil matters in the registers of the police. The daily guards in time of peace, the advanced guards and outposts in time of war, which are mounted regularly by the centuries and messes in their turns, are likewise punctually kept in rolls for that purpose, with the name of each soldier whose tour is past, that no one may have injustice done him or be excused from his duty by favor.

They are also exact in entering the time and limitation of furloughs, which formerly were never granted without difficulty and only on real and urgent business. They then never suffered the soldiers to attend on any private person or to concern themselves in private occupations, thinking it absurd and improper that the Emperor's soldiers, clothed and subsisted at the public expense, should follow any other profession. Some soldiers, however, were allowed for the service of the praefects, tribunes and even of the other officers, our of the number of the accensi or such as were raised after the legion was complete. These latter are now called supernumeraries. The regular troops were obliged to carry their wood, hay, water and straw into the camp themselves. From such kind of services they were called munifices.

SOLDIER'S DEPOSITS

The institution of the ancients which obliged the soldiers to deposit half of every donative they received at the colors was wise and judicious; the intent was to preserve it for their use so that they might not squander it in extravagance or idle expense. For most men, particularly the poorer sort, soon spend whatever they can get. A reserve of this kind therefore is evidently of the greatest service to the soldiers themselves; since they are maintained at the public expense, their military stock by this method is continually increasing. The soldier who knows all his fortune is deposited at his colors, entertains no thoughts of desertion, conceives a greater affection for them and fights with greater intrepidity in their defense. He is also prompted thereto by interest, the most prevailing consideration among men. This money was contained in ten bags, one for each cohort. There was an eleventh bag also for a small contribution from the whole legion, as a common fund to defray the expense of burial of any of their deceased comrades. These collections were kept in baskets in the custody of the ensigns, chosen for their integrity and capacity, and answerable for the trust and obliged to account with every man for his own proportion.

PROMOTION IN THE LEGION

Heaven certainly inspired the Romans with the organization of the legion, so superior does it seem to human invention. Such is the arrangement and disposition of the ten cohorts that compose it, as to appear one perfect body and form one complete whole. A soldier, as he advances in rank, proceeds as it were by rotation through the different degrees of the several cohorts in such a manner that one who is promoted passes from the first cohort to the tenth, and returns again regularly through all the others with a continual increase of rank and pay to the first. Thus the centurion of the primiple, after having commanded in the different ranks of every cohort, attains that great dignity in the first with infinite advantages from the whole legion. The chief praefect of the Praetorian Guards rises by the same method of rotation to that lucrative and honorable rank. Thus the legionary horse contract an affection for the foot of their own cohorts, notwithstanding the natural antipathy existing between the two corps. And this connection establishes a reciprocal attachment and union between all the cohorts and the cavalry and infantry of the legion.

LEGIONARY MUSIC

The music of the legion consists of trumpets, cornets and buccinae. The trumpet sounds the charge and the retreat. The cornets are used only to regulate the motions of the colors; the trumpets serve when the soldiers are ordered out to any work without the colors; but in time of action, the trumpets and cornets sound together. The classicum, which is a particular sound of the buccina or horn, is appropriated to the commander-in-chief and is used in the presence of the general, or at the execution of a soldier, as a mark of its being done by his authority. The ordinary guards and outposts are always mounted and relieved by the sound of trumpet, which also directs the motions of the soldiers on working parties and on field days. The cornets sound whenever the colors are to be struck or planted. These rules must be punctually observed in all exercises and reviews so that the soldiers may be ready to obey them in action without hesitation according to the general's orders either to charge or halt, to pursue the enemy or to retire. F or reason will convince us that what is necessary to be performed in the heat of action should constantly be practiced in the leisure of peace.

THE DRILLING OF THE TROOPS

The organization of the legion being thus explained, let us return to the drills. The younger soldiers and recruits went through their drills of every kind every morning and afternoon and the veterans and most expert regularly once a day. Length of service or age alone will never form a military man, for after serving many years an undisciplined soldier is still a novice in his profession. Not only those under the masters at arms, but all the soldiers in general, were formerly trained incessantly in those drills which now are only exhibited as shows in the circus for particular solemnities. By practice only can be acquired agility of body and the skill requisite to engage an enemy with advantage, especially in close fight. But the most essential point of all is to teach soldiers to keep their ranks and never abandon their colors in the most difficult evolutions. Men thus trained are never at a loss amidst the greatest confusion of numbers.

The recruits likewise are to be exercised with wooden swords at the post, to be taught to attack this imaginary antagonist on all sides and to aim at the sides, feet or head, both with the point and edge of the sword. They must be instructed how to spring forward to give the blow, to rise with a bound above the shield and then to sink down and shelter themselves under cover of it, and how to advance and retire. They must also throw their javelins at the post from a considerable distance in order to acquire a good aim and strengthen the arm.

The archers and slingers set up bundles of twigs or straw for marks, and generally strike them with arrows and with stones from the fustiablus at the distance of six hundred feet. They acquired coolness and exactness in acnon from familiar custom and exercise in the field. The slingers should be taught to whirl the sling but once about the head before they cast the stone. Formerlyall soldiers were trained to the praccice of throwing stones of a pound weight with the hand, as this was thought a readier method since it did not require a sling. The use of the common missile weapons and loaded javelins was another part of the drill strictly attended to.

To continue this drill without interruption during the winter, they erected for the cavalry porticos or riding halls covered with tiles or shingles, and if they were not to be procured, with reeds, rushes or thatch. Large open halls were likewise constructed in the same manner for the use of the infantry. By these means the troops were provided with places of drill sheltered from bad weather. But even in winter, if it did not rain or snow, they were obliged to perform their drills in the field, lest an intermission of discipline should affect both the courage and constitution of the soldier. In short, both legionary and auxiliary troops should continually be drilled in cutting wood, carrying burdens, passing ditches, swimming in the sea or in rivers, marching in the full step and even running with their arms and baggage, so that, inured to labor in peace, they may find no difficulty in war. For, as the well trained soldier is eager for action, so does the untaught fear it. In war discipline is superior to strength; but if that discipline is neglected, there is no longer any difference between the soldier and the peasant. The old maxim is certain that the very essence of an art consists in constant practice.

MACHINES AND TOOLS OF THE LEGION

The legion owes its success to its arms and machines, as well as to the number and bravery of its soldiers. In the first place every century has a balista mounted on a carriage drawn by mules and served by a mess, that is by ten men from the century to which it belongs. The larger these engines are, the greater distance they carry and with the greater force. They are used not only to defend the entrenchments of camps, but are also placed in the field in the rear of the heavy armed infantry. And such is the violence with which they throw the darts that neither the cuirasses of the horse nor shields of the foot can resist them. The number of these engines in a legion is fiftyfive. Besides these are ten onagri, one for each cohort; they are drawn ready armed on carriages by oxen; in case of an attack, they defend the works of the camp by throwing stones as the balistae do darts.

The legion carries with it a number of small boats, each hollowed out of a single piece of timber, with long cables and sometimes iron chains to fasten them together. These boats, joined and covered with planks, serve as bridges over unfordable rivers, on which both cavalry and infantry pass without danger. The legion is provided with iron hooks, called wolves, and iron scythes fixed to the ends of long poles; and with forks, spades, shovels, pickaxes, wheelbarrows and baskets for digging and transporting earth; together with hatchets, axes and saws for cutting wood. Besides which, a train of workmen attend on it furnished with all instruments necessary for the construction of tortoises, musculi, rams, vines, moving towers and other machines for the attack of places. As the enumeration of all the particulars of this sort would be too tedious, I shall only observe that the legion should carry with it wherever it moves, whatever is necessary for every kind of service so that the encampments may have all the strength and conveniences of a fortified city.

Preface to Book III

To the Emperor Valentinian

The Athenians and Lacedaemonians were masters of Greece before the Macedonians, as history informs us. The Athenians excelled not only in war but in other arts and sciences. The Lacedaemonians made war their chief study. They are affirmed to be the first who reasoned on the events of battles and committed their observations thereon to writing with such success as to reduce the military art, before considered as totally dependent on courage or fortune, to certain rules and fixed principles. As a consequence they established schools of tactics for the instruction of youth in all the maneuvers of war. How worthy of admiration are these people for particularly applying themselves to the study of an art, without which no other art can possibly exist. The Romans followed their example, and both practiced their institutions in their armies and preserved them in their writings. These are the maxims and instructions dispersed through the works of different authors, which Your Majesty has ordered me to abridge, since the perusal of the whole would be too tedious, and the authority of only a part unsatisfactory. The effect of the Lacedaemonian skill in dispositions for general actions appears evidently in the single instance of Xantippus, who assisted the Carthaginians after the repeated ruin of their armies. And merely superior skill and conduct defeated Attilius Regulus at the head of a Roman army, till that time always victorious. Xantippus took him prisoner and thus terminated the war by a single action. Hannibal, also, before he set out on his expedition into Italy, chose a Lacedaemonian for his counsellor in military operations; and by his advice, though inferior to the

Romans both in number and strength, overthrew so many consuls and such mighty legions. He, therefore, who desires peace, should prepare for war. He who aspires to victory, should spare no pains to form his soldiers. And he who hopes for success, should fight on principle, not chance. No one dares to offend or insult a power of known superiority in action.

Book III: Dispositions for Action

THE NUMBER WHICH SHOULD COMPOSE AN ARMY

The first book treats of the choice and exercises of new levies; the second explains the establishment of the legion and the method of discipline; and the third contains the dispositions for action. By this methodical progression, the following instructions on general actions and means of victory will be better understood and of greater use. By an army is meant a number of troops, legions and auxiliaries, cavalry and infantry, assembled to make war. This number is limited by judges of the profession. The defeats of Xerxes, Darius, Mithridates and other monarchs who brought innumerable multitudes into the field, plainly show that the destruction of such prodigious armies is owing more to their own numbers than to the bravery of their enemies. An army too numerous is subject to many dangers and inconveniences. Its bulk makes it slow and unwieldy in its motions; and as it is obliged to march in columns of great length, it is exposed to the risk of being continually harassed and insulted by inconsiderable parties of the enemy. The incumbrance of the baggage is often an occasion of its being surprised in its passage through difficult places or over rivers. The difficulty of providing forage for such numbers of horses and other beasts of burden is very great. Besides, scarcity of provisions, which is to be carefully guarded against in all expeditions, soon ruins such large armies where the consumption is so prodigious, that notwithstanding the greatest care in filling the magazines they must begin to fail in a short time. And sometimes they unavoidably will be distressed for want of water. But, if unfortunately this immense army should be defeated, the numbers lost must necessarily be very great, and the remainder, who save themselves by flight, too much dispirited to be brought again to action.

The ancients, taught by experience, preferred discipline to numbers. In wars of lesser importance they thought one legion with auxiliaries, that is, ten thousand foot and two thousand horse, sufficient. And they often gave the command to a praeter as to a general of the second rank. When the preparations of the enemy were formidable, they sent a general of consular dignity with twenty thousand foot and four thousand horse. In our times this command was given to a count of the first order. But when there happened any dangerous insurrection supported by infinite multitudes of fierce and barbarous nations, on such emergencies they took the field with two armies under two consuls, who were charged, both singly and jointly, to take care to preserve the Republic from danger. In short, by this management, the Romans, almost continually engaged in war with different nations in different parts of the world, found themselves able to oppose them in every quarter. The excellence of their discipline made their small armies sufficient to encounter all their enemies with success. But it was an invariable rule in their armies that the number of allies or auxiliaries should never exceed that of the Roman citizens.

MEANS OF PRESERVING IT IN HEALTH

The next article is of the greatest importance: the means of preserving the health of the troops. This depends on the choice of situation and water, on the season of the year, medicine, and exercise. As to the situation, the army should never continue in the neighborhood of unwholesome marshes any length of time, or on dry plains or eminences without some sort of shade or shelter. In the summer, the troops should never encamp without tents. And their marches, in that season of the year when the heat is excessive, should begin by break of day so that they may arrive at the place of destination in good time. Otherwise they will contract diseases from the heat of the weather and the fatigue of the march. In severe winter they should never march in the night in frost and snow, or be exposed to want of wood or clothes. A soldier, starved with cold, can neither be healthy nor fit for service. The water must be wholesome and not marshy. Bad water is a kind of poison and the cause of epidemic distempers.

It is the duty of the officers of the legion, of the tribunes, and even of the commander-in-chief himself, to take care that the sick soldiers are supplied with proper diet and diligently attended by the physicians. For little can be expected from men who have both the enemy and diseases to struggle with. However, the best judges of the service have always been of the opinion that daily practice of the military exercises is much more efficacious towards the health of an army than all the art of medicine. For this reason they exercised their infantry without intermission. If it rained or snowed, they performed under cover; and ill fine weather, in the field. They also were assiduous in exercising their cavalry, not only in plains, but also on uneven ground, broken and cut with ditches. The horses as well as the men were thus trained, both on the above mentioned account and to prepare them for action. Hence we may perceive the importance and necessity of a strict observance of the military exercises in an army, since health in the camp and victory in the field depend on them. If a numerous army continues long in one place in the summer or in the autumn, the waters become corrupt and the air infected. Malignant and fatal distempers proceed from this and can be avoided only by frequent changes of encampments.

CARE TO PROVIDE FORAGE AND PROVISIONS

Famine makes greater havoc in an army than the enemy, and is more terrible than the sword. Time and opportunity may help to retrieve other misfortunes, but where forage and provisions have not been carefully provided, the evil is without remedy. The main and principal point in war is to secure plenty of provisions and to destroy tIle enemy by famine. An exact calculation must therefore be made before the commencement of the war as to the number of troops and the expenses incident thereto, so that the provinces may in plenty of time furnish the forage, corn, and all other kinds of provisions demanded of them to be transported. They must be in more than sufficient quantity, and gathered into the strongest and most convenient cities before the opening of the campaign. If the provinces cannot raise their quotas in kind, they must commute for them in money to be employed in procuring all things requisite for the service. For the possessions of the subjects cannot be kept secure otherwise than by the defense of arms.

These precautions often become doubly necessary as a siege is sometimes protracted beyond expectation, the besiegers resolving to suffer themselves all the inconveniences of want sooner than raise the siege, if they have any hopes of reducing the place by famine. Edicts should be issued out requiring the country people to convey their cattle, grain, wine and all kinds of provisions that may be of service to the enemy, into garrisoned fortresses or into the safest cities. And if they do not comply with the order, proper officers are to appointed to compel them to do it. The inhabitants of the province must likewise be obliged to retire with their effects into some fortified place before the irruption of the enemy. The fortifications and all the machines of different kinds must also be examined and repaired in time. For if you are once surprised by the enemy before you are in a proper posture of defense, you are thrown into irrecoverable confusion, and you can no longer draw any assistance from the neighboring places, all communication with them being cut off. But a faithful management of the magazines and a frugal distribution of the provisions, with proper precautions taken at first, will insure sufficient plenty. When provisions once begin to fail, parsimony is ill-timed and comes too late.

On difficult expeditions the ancients distributed the provisions at a fixed allowance to each man without distinction of rank; and when the emergency was past, the government accounted for the full proportions. The troops should never want wood and forage in winter or water in summer. They should have corn, wine, vinegar, and even salt, in plenty at all times. Cities and fortresses are garrisoned by such men as are least fit for the service of the field. They are provided with all sorts of arms, arrows, fustibali, slings, stones, onagri and balistae for their defense. Great caution is requisite that the unsuspecting simplicity of the inhabitants be not imposed on by the treachery or perjury of the enemy, for pretended conferences and deceitful appearance of truces have often been more fatal than force. By observing the foregoing precautions, the besieged may have it in their power to ruin the enemy by famine, if he keeps his troops together, and if he divides.them, by frequent sallies and surprises.

METHODS TO PREVENT MUTINY IN AN ARMY

An army drawn together from different parts sometimes is disposed to mutiny. And the troops, though not inclined to fight, pretend to be angry at not being led against the enemy. Such seditious dispositions principally show themselves in those who have lived in their quarters in idleness and effeminacy. These men, unaccustomed to the necessary fatigue of the field, are disgusted at its severity. Their ignorance of discipline makes them afraid of action and inspires them with insolence.

There are several remedies for this evil. While the troops are yet separated and each corps continues in its respective quarters, let the tribunes, their lieutenants and the officers in genera4 make it their business to keep up so strict a discipline as to leave them no room to harbor any thoughts but of submission and obedience. Let them be constantly employed either in field days or in the inspection of their arms. They should not be allowed to be absent on furlough. They should be frequently called by roll and trained to be exact in the observance of every signal. Let them be exercised in the use of the bow, in throwing missile weapons and stones, both with the hand and sling, and with the wooden sword at the post; let all this be continually repeated and let them be often kept under arms till they are tired. Let them be exercised in running and leaping to facilitate the passing of ditches. And if their quarters are near the sea or a river, let them all, without exception, be obliged in the summer to have the frequent practice of swimming. Let them be accustomed to march through thickets, inclosures and broken grounds, to fell trees and cut out timber, to break ground and to defend a post against their comrades who are to endeavor to dispossess them; and in the encounter each party should use their shields to dislodge and bear down their antagonists. All the different kinds of troops thus trained and exercised in their quarters will find themselves inspired with emulation for glory and eagerness for action when they come to take the field. In short, a soldier who has proper confidence in his own skill and strength, entertains no thought of mutiny.

A general should be attentive to discover the turbulent and seditious soldiers in the army, legions or auxiliaries, cavalry or infantry. He should endeavor to procure his intelligence not from informers, but from the tribunes, their lieutenants and other officers of undoubted veracity. It would then be prudent in him to separate them from the rest under pretence of some service agreeable to them, or detach them to garrison cities or castles, but with such address that though he wants to get rid of them, they may think themselves employed by preference and favor. A multitude never broke out into open sedition at once and with unanimous consent. They are prepared and excited by some few mutineers, who hope to secure impunity for their crimes by the number of their associates. But if the height of the mutiny requires violent remedies, it will be most advisable, after the manner of the ancients, to punish the ring-leaders only in order that, though few suffer, all may be terrified by the example. But it is much more to the credit of a general to form his troops to submission and obedience by habit and discipline than to be obliged to force them to their duty by the terror of punishment.

MARCHES IN THE NEIGHBORHOOD OF THE ENEMY

It is asserted by those who have made the profession their study that an army is exposed to more danger on marches than in battles. In an engagement the men are properly armed, they see their enemies before them and come prepared to fight. But on a march the soldier is less on his guard, has not his arms always ready and is thrown into disorder by a sudden attack or ambuscade. A general, therefore, cannot be too careful and diligent in taking necessary precautions to prevent a surprise on the march and in making proper dispositions to repulse the enemy, in case of such accident, without loss.

In the first place, he should have an exact description of the country that is. the seat of war, in which the distances of places specified by the number of miles, the nature of the roads, the shortest routes, by-roads, mountains and rivers, should be correctly inserted. We are told that the greatest generals have carried their precautions on this head so far that, not satisfied with the simple description of the country wherein they were engaged, they caused plans to be taken of it on the spot, that they might regulate their marches by the eye with greater safety. A general should also inform himself of all these particulars from persons of sense and reputation well acquainted with the country by examining them separately at first, and then comparing their accounts in order to come at the truth with certainty.

If any difficulty arises about the choice of roads, he should procure proper and skillful guides. He should put them under a guard and spare neither promises nor threat to induce them to be faithful. They will acquit themselves well when they know it is impossible to escape and are certain of being rewarded for their fidelity or punished for their perfidy. He must be sure of their capacity and experience, that the whole army be not brought into danger by the errors of two or three persons. For sometimes the common sort of people imagine they know what they really do not, and through ignorance promise more than they can perform.

But of all precautions the most important is to keep entirely secret which way or by what route the army is to march. For the security of an expedition depends on the concealment of all motions from the enemy. The figure of the Minotaur was anciently among the legionary ensigns, signifying that this monster, according to the fable, was concealed in the most secret recesses and windings of the labyrinth, just as the designs of a general should always be impenetrable. When the enemy has no intimation of a march, it is made with security; but as sometimes the scouts either suspect or discover the decampment, or traitors or deserters give intelligence thereof, it will be proper to mention the method of acting in case of an attack on the march.

The general, before he puts his troops in motion, should send out detachments of trusty and experienced soldiers well mounted, to reconnoiter the places through which he is to march, in front, in rear, and on the right and left, lest he should fall into ambuscades. The night is safer and more advantageous for your spies to do their business in than day, for if they are taken prisoners, you have, as it were, betrayed yourself. After this, the cavalry should march off first, then the infantry; the baggage, bat horses, servants and carriages follow in the center; and part of the best cavalry and infantry come in the rear, since it is oftener attacked on a march than the front. The flanks of the baggage, exposed to frequent ambuscades, must also be covered with a sufficient guard to secure them. But above all, the part where the enemy is most expected must be reinforced with some of the best cavalry, light infantry and foot archers.

If surrounded on all sides by the enemy, you must make dispositions to receive them wherever they come, and the soldiers should be cautioned beforehand to keep their arms in their hands, and to be ready in order to prevent the bad effects of a sudden attack. Men are frightened and thrown into disorder by sudden accidents and surprises of no consequence when foreseen. The ancients were very careful that the servants or followers of the army, if wounded or frightened by the noise of the action, might not disorder the troops while engaged, and also to prevent their either straggling or crowding one another too much, which might incommode their own men and give advantage to the enemy. They ranged the baggage, therefore, in the same manner as the regular troops under particular ensigns. They selected from among the servants the most proper and experienced and gave them the command of a number of servants and boys, not exceeding two hundred, and their ensigns directed them where to assemble the baggage. Proper intervals should always be kept between the baggage and the troops, that the latter may not be embarrassed for want of room in case of an attack during the march. The manner and disposition of defense must be varied according to the difference of ground. In an open country you are more liable to be attacked by horse than foot. But in a woody, mountainous or marshy situation, the danger to be apprehended is from foot. Some of the divisions being apt through negligence to move too fast, and others too slow, great care is to be taken to prevent the army from being broken or from running into too great a length, as the enemy would instantly take advantage of the neglect and penetrate without difficulty.

The tribunes, their lieutenants or the masters at arms of most experience, must therefore be posted at proper distances, in order to halt those who advance too fast and quicken such as move too slow. The men at too great a distance in the front, on the appearance of an enemy, are more disposed to fly than to join their comrades. And those too far behind, destitute of assistance, fall a sacrifice to the enemy and their own despair. The enemy, it may be concluded, will either plant ambuscades or make his attack by open force, according to the advantage of the ground. Circumspection in examining every place will be a security against concealed danger; and an ambuscade, if discovered and promptly surrounded, will return the intended mischief with interest.

If the enemy prepare to fall upon you by open force in a mountainous country, detachments must be sent forward to occupy the highest eminences, so that on their arrival they may not dare to attack you under such a disadvantage of ground, your troops being posted so much above their and presenting a front ready for their reception. It is better to send men forward with hatchets and other tools in order to open ways that are narrow but safe, without regard to the labor, rather than to run any risk in the finest roads. It is necessary to be well acquainted whether the enemy usually make their attempts in the night, at break of day or in the hours of refreshment or rest; and by knowledge of their customs to guard against what we find their general practice. We must also inform ourselves whether they are strongest in infantry or cavalry; whether their cavalry is chiefly armed with lances or with bows; and whether their principal strength consists in their numbers or the excellence of their arms. All of this will enable us to take the most proper measures to distress them and for our advantage. When we have a design in view, we must consider whether it will be most advisable to begin the march by day or by night; we must calculate the distance of the places we want to reach; and take such precautions that in summer the troops may not suffer for want of water on their march, nor be obstructed in winter by impassable morasses or torrents, as these would expose the army to great danger before it could arrive at the place of its destination. As it highly concerns us to guard against these inconveniences with prudence, so it would be inexcusible not to take advantage of an enemy that fell into them through ignorance or negligence. Our spies should be constantly abroad; we should spare no pains in tampering with their men, and give all manner of encouragement to deserters. By these means we may get intelligence of their present or future designs. And we should constantly keep in readiness some detachments of cavalry and light infantry, to fall upon them when they least expect it, either on the march, or when foraging or marauding.

PASSAGES OF RIVERS

The passages of rivers are very dangerous without great precaution. In crossing broad or rapid streams, the baggage, servants, and sometimes the most indolent soldiers are in danger of being lost. Having first sounded the ford, two lines of the best mounted cavalry are ranged at a convenient distance entirely across the river, so that the infantry and baggage may pass between them. The line above the ford breaks the violence of the stream, and the line below recovers and transports the men carried away by the current. When the river is too deep to be forded either by the cavalry or infantry, the water is drawn off, if it runs in a plain, by cutting a great number of trenches, and thus it is passed with ease.

Navigable rivers are passed by means of piles driven into the bottom and floored with planks; or in a sudden emergency by fastening together a number of empty casks and covering them with boards. The cavalry, throwing off their accoutrements, make small floats of dry reeds or rushes on which they lay their rams and cuirasses to preserve them from being wet. They themselves swim their horses across the river and draw the floats after them by a leather thong.

But the most commodious invention is that of the small boats hollowed out of one piece of timber and very light both by their make and the quality of the wood. The army always has a number of these boats upon carriages, together with a sufficient quantity of planks and iron nails. Thus with the help of cables to lash the boats together, a bridge is instantly constructed, which for the time has the solidity of a bridge of stone.

As the enemy generally endeavor to fall upon an army at the passage of a river either by surprise or ambuscade, it is necessary to secure both sides thereof by strong detachments so that the troops may not be attacked and defeated while separated by the channel of the river. But it is still safer to palisade both the posts, since this will enable you to sustain any attempt without much loss. If the bridge is wanted, not only for the present transportation of the troops but also for their return and for convoys, it will be proper to throw up works with large ditches to cover each head of the bridge, with a sufficient number of men to defend them as long as the circumstances of affairs require.

RULES FOR ENCAMPING AN ARMY

An army on the march cannot expect always to find walled cities for quarters, and it is very imprudent and dangerous to encamp in a straggling manner without some sort of entrenchment. It is an easy matter to surprise troops while refreshing themselves or dispersed in the different occupations of the service. The darkness of night, the necessity of sleep and the dispersion of the horses at pasture afford opportunities of surprise. A good situation for a camp is not sufficient; we must choose the very best that can be found lest, having failed to occupy a more advantageous post the enemy should get possession of it to our great detriment.

An army should not encamp in summer near bad waters or far from good ones, nor in winter in a situation without plenty of forage and wood. The camp should not be liable to sudden inundations. The avenues should not be too steep and narrow lest, if invested, the troops should find it difficult to make their retreat; nor should it be commanded by any eminences from which it may be annoyed by the enemy's weapons. After these precautions, the camp is formed square, round, triangular or oblong, according to the nature of the ground. For the form of a camp does not constitute its goodness. Those camps, however, are thought best where the length is one third more than the depth. The dimensions must be exactly computed by the engineers, so that the size of the camp may be proportioned to the number of troops. A camp which is too confined will not permit the troops to perform their movements with freedom, and one which is too extensive divides them too much. There are three methods of entrenching a camp. The first is for the case when the army is on the march and will continue in the camp for only one night. They then throw up a slight parapet of turf and plant it with a row of palisades or caltrops* of wood. The sods are cut with iron instruments. If the earth is held strongly together by the roots of the grass, they are cut in the form of a brick a foot and one half high, a foot broad and a foot and one half long. If the earth is so loose that the turf cannot be cut in this form, they run a slight trench round the camp, five feet broad and three feet deep. The earth taken from the trench forms a parapet on the inside and this secures the army from danger. This is the second method.

But permanent camps, either for summer or winter, in the neighborhood of an enemy, are fortified with greater care and regularity. After the ground is marked out by the proper officers, each century receives a certain number of feet to entrench. They then range their shields and baggage in a circle about their own colors and, with. out other arms than their swords, open a trench nine, eleven or thirteen feet broad. Or, if they are under great apprehensions of the enemy, they enlarge it to seventeen feet (it being a general rule to observe odd numbers). Within this they construct a rampart with fascines or branches of trees well fastened together with pickets, so that the earth may be better supported. Upon this rampart they raise a parapet with battlements as in the fortifications of a city. The centurions measure the work with rods ten feet long and examine whether every one has properly completed the proportion assigned to him. The tribunes likewise inspect the work and should not leave the place till the whole is finished. And that the workmen may not be suddenly interrupted by the enemy, all the cavalry and that part of the infantry exempted by the privilege of their rank from working, remain in order of battle before the entrenchment to be ready to repel any assault.

The first thing to be done after entrenching the camp, is to plant the ensigns, held by the soldiers in the highest veneration and respect, in their proper places. After this the praetorium is prepared for the general and his lieutenants, and the tents pitched for the tribunes, who have soldiers particularly appointed for that service and to fetch their water, wood, and forage. Then the legions and auxiliaries, cavalry and infantry, have the ground distributed to them to pitch their tents according to the rank of the several corps. Four foot-soldiers of each century and four troopers of each troop are on guard every night. As it seemed impossible for a sentinel to remain a whole night on his post, the watches were divided by the hourglass into four parts, that each man might stand only three hours. All guards are mounted by the sound of trumpet and relieved by the sound of cornet. The tribunes choose proper and trusty men to visit the different posts and report to them whatever they find amiss. This is now a military office and the persons appointed to it are called officers of the rounds.

The cavalry furnish the grand guards at night and the outposts by day. They are relieved every morning and afternoon because of the fatigue of the men and horses. It is particularly incumbent upon the general to provide for the protection of the pastures and of the convoys of grain and other provisions either in camp or garrison, and to secure wood, water and forage against the incursions of the enemy. This can only be effected by posting detachments advantageously in the cines or walled castles on the roads along which the convoys advance. And if no ancient fortifications are to be met with, small forts must be built in proper situations, surrounded with large ditches, for the reception of detachments of horse and foot, so that the convoys will be effectually protected. For an enemy will hardly venture far into a country where he knows his adversary's troops are so disposed as to be ready to encompass him on all sides.

MOTIVES FOR THE PLAN OF OPERATIONS OF A CAMPAIGN

Readers of this military abridgement will perhaps be impatient for instructions relative to general engagements. But they should consider that a battle is commonly decided in two or three hours, after which no further hopes are left for the worsted army. Every plan, therefore, is to be considered, every expedient tried and every method taken before matters are brought to this last extremity. Good officers decline general engagements where the danger is common, and prefer the employment of stratagem and finesse to destroy the enemy as much as possible in detail and intimidate them without exposing our own forces.

I shall insert some necessary instructions on this head collected from the ancients. It is the duty and interest of the general frequently to assemble the most prudent and experienced officers of the different corps of. the army and consult with them on the state both of his own and the enemy's forces. All overconfidence, as most pernicious in its consequences, must be banished from the deliberations. He must examine which has the superiority in numbers, whether his or the adversary's troops are best armed, which are in the best condition, best disciplined and most resolute in emergencies. The state of the cavalry of both armies must be inquired into, but more especially that of the infantry, for the main strength of an army consists of the latter. With respect to the cavalry, he must endeavor to find out in which are the greatest numbers of archers or of troopers armed with lances, which has the most cuirassiers and which the best horses. Lastly he must consider the field of battle and to judge whether the ground is more advantageous for him or his enemy. If strongest in cavalry, we should prefer plains and open ground; if superior in infantry, we should choose a situation full of enclosures, ditches, morasses and woods, and sometimes mountainous. Plenty or scarcity in either army are considerations of no small importance, for famine, according to the common proverb, is an internal enemy that makes more havoc than the sword. But the most material article is to determine whether it is most proper to temporize or to bring the affair to a speedy decision by action. The enemy sometimes expect an expedition will soon be over; and if it is protracted to any length, his troops are either consumed by want,. induced to return home by the desire of seeing their families or, having done nothing considerable in the field, disperse themselves from despair of success. Thus numbers, tired out with fatigue and disgusted with the service, desert, others betray them and many surrender themselves. Fidelity is seldom found in troops disheartened by misfortunes. And in such case an army which was numerous on taking the field insensibly dwindles away to nothing.

It is essential to know the character of the enemy and of their principal officers-whether they be. rash or cautious, enterprising or timid, whether they fight on principle or from chance and whether the nations they have been engaged with were brave or cowardly.

We must know how far to depend upon the fidelity and strength of auxiliaries, how the enemy's troops and our own are affected and which appear most confident of success, a consideration of great effect in raising or depressing the courage of an army. A harangue from the general, especially if he seems under no apprehension himself, may reanimate the soldiers if dejected. Their spirits revive if any considerable advantage is gained either by stratagem or otherwise, if the fortune of the enemy begins to change or if you can contrive to beat some of their weak or poorly-armed detachments.

But you must by no means venture to lead an irresolute or diffident army to a general engagement. The difference is great whether your troops are raw or veterans, whether inured to war by recent service or for some years unemployed. For soldiers unused to fighting for a length of time must be considered in the same light as recruits. As soon as the legions, auxiliaries and cavalry are assembled from their several quarters, it is the duty of a good general to have every corps instructed separately in every part of the drill by tribunes of known capacity chosen for that purpose. He should afterwards form them into one body and train them in all the maneuvers of the line as for a general action. He must frequently drill them himself to try their skill and strength, and to see whether they perform their evolutions with proper regularity and are sufficiently attentive to the sound of the trumpets, the motions of the colors and to his own orders and signals. If deficient in any of these particulars, they must be instructed and exercised till perfect.

But though thoroughly disciplined and complete in their field exercises, in the use of the bow and javelin, and in the evolutions of the line, it is not advisable to lead them rashly or immediately to battle. A favorable opportunity must be watched for, and they must first be prepared by frequent skirmishes and slight encounters. Thus a vigilant and prudent general will carefully weigh in his council the state of his own forces and of those of the enemy, just as a civil magistrate judging between two contending parties. If he finds himself in many respects superior to his adversary, he must by no means defer bringing on an engagement. But if he knows himself inferior, he must avoid general actions and endeavor to succeed by surprises, ambuscades and stratagems. These, when skillfully managed by good generals, have often given them the victory over enemies superior both in numbers and strength.

HOW TO MANAGE RAW AND UNDISCIPLINED TROOPS

All arts and trades whatever are brought to perfection by continual practice. How much more should this maxim, true in inconsiderable matters, be observed in affairs of importance! And how much superior to all others is the art of war, by which our liberties are preserved, our dignities perpetuated and the provinces and the whole Empire itself exist. The Lacedaemonians, and after them the Romans, were so aware of this truth that to this science they sacrificed all others. And the barbarous nations even at this day think only this art worth attention, believing it includes or confers everything else. In short, it is indispensably necessary for those engaged in war not only to instruct them in the means of preserving their own lives, but how to gain the victory over their enemies.

A commander-in-chief therefore, whose power and dignity are so great and to whose fidelity and bravery the fortunes of his countrymen, the defense of their cities, the lives of the soldiers, and the glory of the state, are entrusted, should not only consult the good of the army in general, but extend his care to every private soldier in it. For when any misfortunes happen to those under his command, they are considered as public losses and imputed entirely to his misconduct. If therefore he finds his army composed of raw troops or if they have long been unaccustomed to fighting, he must carefully study the strength, the spirit, the manners of each particular legion, and of each body of auxiliaries, cavalry and infantry. He must know, if possible, the name and capacity of every count, tribune, subaltern and soldier. He must assume the most respectable authority and maintain it by severity. He must punish all military crimes with the greatest rigor of the laws. He must have the character of being inexorable towards offenders and endeavor to give public examples thereof in different places and on different occasions.

Having once firmly established these regulations, he must watch the opportunity when the enemy, dispersed in search of plunder, think themselves in security, and attack them with detachments of tried cavalry or infantry, intermingled with young soldiers, or such as are under the military age. The veterans will acquire fresh experience and the others will be inspired with courage by the advantages such opportunities will give him. He should form ambuscades with the greatest secrecy to surprise the enemy at the passages of rivers, in the rugged passes of mountains, in defiles in woods and when embarrassed by morasses or difficult roads. He should regulate his march so as to fall upon them while taking their refreshments or sleeping, or at a time when they suspect no dangers and are dispersed, unarmed and their horses unsaddled. He should continue these kinds of encounters till his soldiers have imbibed a proper confidence in themselves. For troops that have never been in action or have not for some time been used to such spectacles, are greatly shocked at the sight of the wounded and dying; and the impressions of fear they receive dispose them rather to fly than fight.

If the enemy makes excursions or expeditions, the general should attack him after the fatigue of a long march, fall upon him unexpectedly, or harass his rear. He should detach parties to endeavor to carry off by surprise any quarters established at a distance from the hostile army for the convenience of forage or provisions. F or such measures should be pursued at first as can produce no very bad effects if they should happen to miscarry, but would be of great advantage if attended with success. A prudent general will also try to sow dissention among his adversaries, for no nation, though ever so weak in itself can be completely ruined by its enemies unless its fall be facilitated by its own distraction. In civil dissensions men are so intent on the destruction of their private enemies that they are entirely regardless of the public safety.

One maxim must be remembered throughout this work: that no one should ever despair of effecting what has been already performed. It may be said that our troops for many years past have not even fortified their permanent camps with ditches, ramparts or palisades. The answer is plain. If those precautions had been taken, our armies would never have suffered by surprises of the enemy both by day and night. The Persians, after the example of the old Romans, surround their camps with ditches and, as the ground in their country is generally sandy, they always carry with them empty bags to fill with the sand taken out of the trenches and raise a parapet by piling them one on the other. All the barbarous nations range their carriages round them in a circle, a method which bears some resemblance to a fortified camp. They thus pass their nights secure from surprise.

Are we afraid of not being able to learn from others what they before have learned from us? At present all this is to be found in books only, although formerly constantly practiced. Inquiries are now no longer made about customs that have been so long neglected, because in the midst of peace, war is looked upon as an object too distant to merit consideration. But former instances will convince us that the reestablishment of ancient discipline is by no means impossible, although now so totally lost.

In former ages the art of war, often neglected and forgotten, was as often recovered from books and reestablished by the authority and attention of our generals. Our armies in Spain, when Scipio Africanus took the command, were in bad order and had often been beaten under preceding generals. He soon reformed them by severe discipline and obliged them to undergo the greatest fatigue in the different military works, reproaching them that since they would not wet their hands with the blood of their enemies, they should soil them with the mud of the trenches. In short, with these very troops he afterwards took the city of Numantia and burned it to the ground with such destruction of its inhabitants that not one escaped. In Africa an army, which under the command of Albinus had been forced to pass under the yoke, was by Metellus brought into such order and discipline, by forming it on the ancient model, that they afterwards vanquished those very enemies who had subjected them to that ignominious treatment. The Cimbri defeated the legions of Caepio, Manilus and Silanus in Gaul, but Marius collected their shattered remnants and disciplined them so effectually that he destroyed an innumerable multitude of the Cimbri, Teutones and Ambrones in one general engagement. Nevertheless it is easier to form young soldiers and inspire them with proper notions of honor than to reanimate troops who have been once disheartened.

PREPARATIONS FOR A GENERAL ENGAGEMENT

Having explained the less considerable branches of the art of war, the order of military affairs naturally leads us to the general engagement. This is a conjuncture full of uncertainty and fatal to kingdoms and nations, for in the decision of a pitched battle consists the fulness of victory. This eventuality above all others requires the exertion of all the abilities of a general, as his good conduct on such an occasion gains him greater glory, or his dangers expose him to greater danger and disgrace. This is the moment in which his talents, skill and experience show themselves in their fullest extent.

Formerly to enable the soldiers to charge with greater vigor, it was customary to order them a moderate refreshment of food before an engagement, so that their strength might be the better supported during a long conflict. When the army is to march out of a camp or city in the presence of their enemies drawn up and ready for action, great precaution must be observed lest they should be attacked as they defile from the gates and be cut to pieces in detail. Proper measures must therefore be taken so that the whole army may be clear of the gates and form in order of battle before the enemy's approach. If they are ready before you can have quitted the place, your design of marching out must either be deferred till another opportunity or at least dissembled, so that when they begin to insult you on the supposition that you dare not appear, or think of nothing but plundering or returning and no longer keep their ranks, you may sally out and fall upon them while in confusion and surprise. Troops must never be engaged in a general action immediately after a long march, when the men are fatigued and the horses tired. The strength required for action is spent in the toil of the march. What can a soldier do who charges when out of breath? The ancients carefully avoided this inconvenience, but in later times some of our Roman generals, to say nothing more, have lost their armies by unskillfully neglecting this precaution. Two armies, one tired and spent, the other fresh and in full vigor, are by no means an equal match.

THE SENTIMENTS OF THE TROOPS SHOULD BE DETERMINED BEFORE BATTLE

It is necessary to know the sentiments of the soldiers on the day of an engagement. Their confidence or apprehensions are easily discovered by their looks, their words, their actions and their motions. No great dependence is to be placed on the eagerness of young soldiers for action, for fighting has something agreeable in the idea to those who are strangers to it. On the other hand, it would be wrong to hazard an engagement, if the old experienced soldiers testify to a disinclination to fight. A general, however, may encourage and animate his troops by proper exhortations and harangues, especially if by his account of the approaching action he can persuade them into the belief of an easy victory. With this view, he should lay before them the cowardice or unskillfulness of their enemies and remind them of any former advantages they may have gained over them. He should employ every argument capable of exciting rage, hatred and indignation against the adversaries in the minds of his soldiers.

It is natural for men in general to be affected with some sensations of fear at the beginning of an engagement, but there are without doubt some of a more timorous disposition who are disordered by the very sight of the enemy. To diminish these apprehensions before you venture on action, draw up your army frequently in order of battle in some safe situation, so that your men may be accustomed to the sight and appearance of the enemy. When opportunity offers, they should be sent to fall upon them and endeavor to put them to flight or kill some of their men. Thus they will become acquainted with their customs, arms and horses. And the objects with which we are once familiarized are no longer capable of inspiring us with terror.

CHOICE OF THE FIELD OF BATTLE

Good generals are acutely aware that victory depends much on the nature of the field of battle. When you intend therefore to engage, endeavor to draw the chief advantage from your situation. The highest ground is reckoned the best. Weapons thrown from a height strike with greater force; and the party above their antagonists can repulse and bear them down with greater impetuosity, while they who struggle with the ascent have both the ground and the enemy to contend with. There is, however, this difference with regard to place: if you depend on your foot against the enemy's horse, you must choose a rough, unequal and mountainous situation. But if, on the contrary, you expect your cavalry to act with advantage against the enemy's infantry, your ground must indeed be higher, but plain and open, without any obstructions of woods or morasses.

ORDER OF BATTLE

In drawing up an army in order of battle, three things are to be considered: the sun, the dust and the wind. The sun in your face dazzles the sight: if the wind is against you, it turns aside and blunts the force of your weapons, while it assists those of your adversary; and the dust driving in your front fills the eyes of your men and blinds them. Even the most unskillful endeavor to avoid these inconveniences in the moment of making their dispositions; but a prudent general should extend his views beyond the present; he should talke such measures as not to be incommoded in the course of the day by different aspects of the sun or by contrary winds which often rise at a certain hour and might be detrimental during action. Our troops should be so disposed as to have these inconveniences behind them, while they are directly in the enemy's front.

PROPER DISTANCES AND INTERVALS

Having explained the general disposition of the lines, we now come to the distances and dimensions. One thousand paces contain a single rank of one thousand six hundred and fifty-six foot soldiers, each man being allowed three feet. Six ranks drawn up on the same extent of ground will require nine thousand nine hundred and ninety-six men. To form only three ranks of the same number will take up two thousand paces, but it is much better to increase the number of ranks than to make your front too extensive. We have before observed the distance between each rank should be six feet, one foot of which is taken up by the men. Thus if you form a body of ten thousand men into six ranks they will occupy thirty-six feet. in depth and a thousand paces in front. By this calculation it is easy to compute the extent of ground required for twenty or thirty thousand men to form upon. Nor can a general be mistaken when thus he knows the proportion of ground for any fixed number of men.

But if the field of battle is not spacious enough or your troops are very numerous, you may form them into nine ranks or even more, for it is more advantageous to engage in close order that to extend your line too much. An army that takes up too much ground in front and too little in depth, is quickly penetrated by the enemy's first onset. After this there is no remedy. As to the post of the different corps in the right or left wing or in the center, it is the general rule to draw them up according to their respective ranks or to distribute them as circumstances or the dispositions of the enemy may require.

DISPOSITION OF THE CAVALRY

The line of infantry being formed, the cavalry are drawn up in the wings. The heavy horse, that is, the cuirassiers and troopers armed with lances, should join the infantry. The light cavalry, consisting of the archers and those who have no cuirasses, should be placed at a greater distance. The best and heaviest horse are to cover the flanks of the foot, and the light horse are posted as abovementioned to surround and disorder the enemy's wings. A general should know what part of his own cavalry is most proper to oppose any particular squadrons or troops of the enemy. For from some causes not to be accounted for some particular corps fight better against others, and those who have defeated superior enemies are often overcome by an inferior force.

If your cavalry is not equal to the enemy's it is proper, after the ancient custom, to intermingle it with light infantry armed with small shields and trained to this kind of service. By observing this method, even though the flower of the enemy's cavalry should attack you, they will never be able to cope with this mixed disposition. This was the only resource of the old generals to supply the defects of their cavalry, and they intermingled the men, used to running and armed for this purpose with light shields, swords and darts, among the horse, placing one of them between two troopers.

RESERVES

The method of having bodies of reserves in rear of the army, composed of choice infantry and cavalry, commanded by the supernumerary lieutenant generals, counts and tribunes, is very judicious and of great consequence towards the gaining of a battle. Some should be posted in rear of the wings and some near the center, to be ready to fly immediately to the assistance of any part of the line which is hard pressed, to prevent its being pierced, to supply the vacancies made therein during the action and thereby to keep up the courage of their fellow soldiers and check the impetuosity of the enemy. This was an invention of the Lacedaemonians, in which they were imitated by the Carthaginians. The Romans have since observed it, and indeed no better disposition can be found.

The line is solely designed to repulse, or if possible, break the enemy. If it is necessary to form the wedge or the pincers, it must be done by the supernumerary troops stationed in the rear for that purpose. If the saw is to be formed, it must also be done from the reserves, for if once you begin to draw off men from the line you throw all into confusion. If any flying platoon of the enemy should fall upon your wing or any other part of your army, and you have no supernumerary troops to oppose it or if you pretend to detach either horse or foot from your line for that service by endeavoring to protect one part, you will expose the other to greater danger. In armies not very numerous, it is much better to contract the front, and to have strong reserves. In short, you must have a reserve of good and well-armed infantry near the center to form the wedge and thereby pierce the enemy's line; and also bodies of cavalry armed with lances and cuirasses, with light infantry, near the wings, to surround the flanks of the enemy.

THE POST OF THE GENERAL AND OF THE SECOND AND THIRD IN COMMAND

The post of the commander-in-chief is generally on the right between the cavalry and infantry. For from this place he can best direct the motions of the whole army and move elements with the greatest ease wherever he finds it necessary. It is also the most convenient spot to give his orders to both horse and foot and to animate them equally by his presence. It is his duty to surround the enemy's left wing opposed to him with his reserve of horse and light infantry, and attack it in the flank and rear. The second in command is posted in the center of the infantry to encourage and support them. A reserve of good and well-armed infantry is near him and under his orders. With this reserve he either forms the wedge to pierce the enemy's line or, if they form the wedge first, prepares the pincers for its reception. The post of the third in command is on the left. He should be a careful and intrepid officer, this part of the army being difficult to manage and defective, as it were, from its situation in the line. He should therefore have a reserve of good cavalry and active infantry to enable him always to extend his left in such a manner as to prevent its being surrounded.

The war shout should not be begun till both armies have joined, for it is a mark of ignorance or cowardice to give it at a distance. The effect is much greater on the enemy when they find themselves struck at the same instant with the horror of the noise and the points of the weapons.

You must always endeavor to get the start of your enemy in drawing up in order of battle, as you will then have it in your power to make your proper dispositions without obstruction. This will increase the courage of your own troops and intimidate your adversaries. For a superiority of courage seems to be implied on the side of an army that offers battle, whereas troops begin to be fearful who see their enemies ready to attack them. You will also secure another great advantage, that of marching up in order and falling upon them while forming and still in confusion. For part of the victory consists in throwing the enemy into disorder before you engage them.

MANEUVERS IN ACTION

An able general never loses a favorable opportunity of surprising the enemy either when tired on the march, divided in the passage of a river, embarrassed in morasses, struggling with the declivities of mountains, when dispersed over the country they think themselves in security or are sleeping in their quarters. In all these cases the adversaries are surprised and destroyed before they have time to put themselves on their guard. But if they are too cautious to give you an opportunity of surprising or ensnaring them, you are then obliged to engage openly and on equal terms. This at present is foreign to the subject. However military skill is no less necessary in general actions than in carrying on war by subtlety and stratagem.

Your first care is to secure your left wing from being surrounded by the enemy's numbers or attacked in flank or rear by flying platoons, a misfortune that often happens. Nor is your right to be neglected, though less frequently in danger. There is only one remedy for this: to wheel back your wing and throw it into a circular position. By this evolution your soldiers meet the enemy on the quarter attacked and defend the rear of their comrades. But your best men should be posted on the angles of the flanks, since it is against them the enemy make their principal efforts.

There is also a method of resisting the wedge when formed by the enemy. The wedge is a disposition of a body of infantry widening gradually towards the base and terminating in a point towards the front. It pierces the enemy's line by a multitude of darts directed to one particular place. The soldiers call it the swine's head. To oppose this disposition, they make use af another called the pincers, resembling the letter V, composed of a body of men in close order. It receives the wedge, inclosing it on both sides, and thereby prevents it from penetrating the line.

The saw is another disposition formed of resolute soldiers drawn up in a straight line advanced into the front against the enemy, to repair any disorder. The platoon is a body of men separated from the line, to hover on every side and attack the enemy wherever they find opportunity. And against this is to be detached a stronger and more numerous platoon.

Above all, a general must never attempt to alter his dispositions or break his order of battle during the time of action, for such an alteration would immediately Occasion disorder and confusion which the enemy would not fail to improve to their advantage.

VARIOUS FORMATIONS FOR BATTLE

An army may be drawn up for a general engagement in seven different formations. The first formation is an oblong square of a large front, of common use both in ancient and modern times, although not thought the best by various judges of the service, because an even and level plain of an extent sufficient to contain its front cannot always be found, and if there should be any irregularity or hollow in the line, it is often pierced in that part. Besides, an enemy superior in number may surround either your right or left wing, the consequence of which will be dangerous, unless you have a reserve ready to advance and sustain his attack. A general should make use of this disposition only when his forces are better and more numerous than the enemy's, it being thereby in his power to attack both the flanks and surround them on every side.

The second and best disposition is the oblique. For although your army consists of few troops, yet good and advantageously posted, it will greatly contribute to your obtaining the victory, notwithstanding the numbers and bravery of the enemy. It is as follows: as the armies are marching up to the attack, your left wing must be kept back at such a distance from the enemy's right as to be out of reach of their darts and arrows. Your right wing must advance obliquely upon the enemy's left, and begin the engagement. And you must endeavor with your best cavalry and infantry to surround the wing with which you are engaged, make it give way and fall upon the enemy in the rear. If they once give ground and the attack is properly seconded, you will undoubtedly gain the victory, while your left wing, which continued at a distance, will remain untouched. An army drawn up in this manner bears some resemblance to the letter A or a mason's level. If the enemy should be beforehand with you in this evolution, recourse must be had to the supernumerary horse and foot posted as a reserve in the rear, as I mentioned before. They must be ordered to support your left wing. This will enable you to make a vigorous resistance against the artifice of the enemy.

The third formation is like the second, but not so good, as it obliges you to begin the attack with your left wing on the enemy's right. The efforts of soldiers on the left are weak and imperfect from their exposed and defective situation in the line. I will explain this formation more clearly. Although your left wing should be much better than your right, yet it must be reinforced with some of the best horse and foot and ordered to commence the acnon with the enemy's right in order to disorder and surround it as expeditiously as possible. And the other part of your army, composed of the worst troops, should remain at such a distance from the enemy's left as not to be annoyed by their darts or in danger of being attacked sword in hand. In this oblique formation care must be taken to prevent the line being penetrated by the wedges of the enemy, and it is to be employed only when the enemy's right wing is weak and your greatest strength is on your left.

The fourth formation is this: as your army is marching to the attack in order of battle and you come within four or five hundred paces of the enemy, both your wings must be ordered unexpectedly to quicken their pace and advance with celerity upon them. When they find themselves attacked on both wings at the same time, the sudden surprise may so disconcert them as to give you an easy victory. But although this method, if your troops are very resolute and expert, may ruin the enemy at once, yet it is hazardous.

The general who attempts it is obliged to abandon and expose his center and to divide his army into three parts. If the enemy are not routed at the first charge, they have a fair opportunity of attacking the wings which are separated from each other and the center which is destitute of assistance.

The fifth formation resembles the fourth but with this addition: the light infantry and the archers are formed before the center to cover it from the attempts of the enemy. With this precaution the general may safely follow the above mentioned method and attack the enemy's left wing with his right, and their right with his left. If he puts them to flight, he gains an immediate victory, and if he fails of success his center is in no danger, being protected by the light infantry and archers.

The sixth formation is very good and almost like the second. It is used when the general cannot depend either on the number or courage of his troops. If made with judgment, notwithstanding his inferiority, he has often a good chance for victory. As your line approaches the enemy, advance your right wing against their left and begin the attack with your best cavalry and infantry. At the same time keep the rest of the army at a great distance from the enemy's right, extended in a direct line like a javelin. Thus if you can surround their left and attack it in flank and rear, you must inevitably defeat them. It is impossible for the enemy to draw off reinforcements from their right or from their center to sustain their left in this emergency, since the remaining part of your army is extended and at a great distance from them in the form of the letter L. It is a formation often used in an action on a march.

The seventh formation owes its advantages to the nature of the ground and will enable you to oppose an enemy with an army inferior both in numbers and goodness, provided one of your flanks can be covered either with an eminence, the sea, a river, a lake, a city, a morass or broken ground inaccessible to the enemy. The rest of the army must be formed, as usual, in a straight line and the unsecured flank must be protected by your light troops and all your cavalry. Sufficiently defended on one side by the nature of the ground and on the other by a double support of cavalry, you may then safely venture on action.

One excellent and general rule must be observed. If you intend to engage with your right wing only, it must be composed of your best troops. And the same method must be taken with respect to the left. Or if you intend to penetrate the enemy's line, the wedges which you form for that purpose before your center, must consist of the best disciplined soldiers. Victory in general is gained by a small number of men. Therefore the wisdom of a general appears in nothing more than in such choice of disposition of his men as is most consonant with reason and service.

THE FLIGHT OF AN ENEMY SHOULD NOT BE PREVENTED, BUT FACILITATED

Generals unskilled in war think a victory incomplete unless the enemy are so straightened in their ground or so entirely surrounded by numbers as to have no possibility of escape. But in such situation, where no hopes remain, fear itself will arm an enemy and despair inspires courage. When men find they must inevitably perish, they willingly resolve to die with their comrades and with their arms in their hands. The maxim of Scipio, that a golden bridge should be made for a flying enemy, has much been commended. For when they have free room to escape they think of nothing but how to save themselves by flight, and the confusion becoming general, great numbers are cut to pieces. The pursuers can be in no danger when the vanquished have thrown away their arms for greater haste. In this case the greater the number of the flying army, the greater the slaughter. Numbers are of no signification where troops once thrown into consternation are equally terrified at the sight of the enemy as at their weapons. But on the contrary, men when shut up, although weak and few in number, become a match for the enemy from this very reflection, that they have no resource but in despair.

"The conquer'd's safety is, to hope for none."

MANNER OF CONDUCTING A RETREAT

Having gone through the various particulars relative to general actions, it remains at present to explain the manner of retreating in presence of the enemy. This is an operation, which, in the judgment of men of greatest skill and experience, is attended with the utmost hazard. A general certainly discourages his own troops and animates his enemies by retiring out of the field without fighting. Yet as this must sometimes necessarily happen, it will be proper to consider how to perform it with safety.

In the first place your men must not imagine that you retire to decline an action, but believe your retreat an artifice to draw the enemy into an ambuscade or more advantageous position where you may easier defeat them in case they follow you. For troops who perceive their general despairs of success are prone to flight. You must be cautious lest the enemy should discover your retreat and immediately fall upon you. To avoid this danger the cavalry are generally posted in the front of the infantry to conceal their motions and retreat from the enemy. The first divisions are drawn off first, the others following in their turns. The last maintain their ground till the rest have marched off, and then file off themselves and join them in a leisurely and regular succession. Some generals have judged it best to make their retreat in the night after reconnoitering their routes, and thus gain so much ground that the enemy, not discovering their departure till daybreak, were not able to come up with them. The light infantry was also sent forward to possess the eminences under which the army might instantly retire with safety; and the enemy, in case they pursued, be exposed to the light infantry, masters of the heights, seconded by the cavalry.

A rash and inconsiderate pursuit exposes an army to the greatest danger possible, that of falling into ambuscades and the hands of troops ready for their reception. For as the temerity of an army is increased and their caution lessened by the pursuit of a flying enemy, this is the most favorable opportunity for such snares. The greater the security, the greater the danger. Troops, when unprepared, at their meals, fatigued after a march, when their horses are feeding, and in short, when they believe themselves most secure, are generally most liable to a surprise. All risks of this sort are to be carefully avoided and all opportunities taken of distressing the enemy by such methods. Neither numbers nor courage avail in misfortunes of this nature.

A general who has been defeated in a pitched battle, although skill and conduct have the greatest share in the decision, may in his defense throw the blame on fortune. But if he has suffered himself to be surprised or drawn into the snares of his enemy, he has no excuse for his fault, because he might have avoided such a misfortune by taking proper precautions and employing spies on whose intelligence he could depend.

When the enemy pursue a retreating foe, the following snare is usually laid. A small body of cavalry is ordered to pursue them on the direct road. At the same time a strong detachment is secretly sent another way to conceal itself on their route. When the cavalry have overtaken the enemy, they make some feint attacks and retire. The enemy, imagining the danger past, and that they have escaped the snare, neglect their order and march without regularity. Then the detachment sent to intercept them, seizing the opportunity, falls upon them unexpectedly and destroys them with ease.

Many generals when obliged to retreat through woods send forward parties to seize the defiles and difficult passes, to avoid ambuscades and block the roads with barricades of felled trees to secure themselves from being pursued and attacked in the rear. In short both sides have equal opportunities of surprising or laying ambuscades on the march. The army which retreats leaves troops behind for that purpose posted in convenient valleys or mountains covered with woods, and if the enemy falls into the snare, it returns immediately to their assistance. The army that pursues detaches different parties of light troops to march ahead through by-roads and intercepts the enemy, who are thus surrounded and attacked at once in front and rear. The flying army may return and fall on the enemy while asleep in the night. And the pursuing army may, even though the distance is great, surprise the adversary by forced marches. The former endeavor may be at the crossing of a river in order to destroy such part of the enemy's army as has already crossed. The pursuers hasten their march to fall upon those bodies of the enemy that have not yet crossed.

ARMED CHARIOTS AND ELEPHANTS

The armed chariots used in war by Antiochus and Mithridates at first terrified the Romans, but they afterwards made a jest of them. As a chariot of this sort does not always meet with plain and level ground, the least obstruction stops it. And if one of the horses be either killed or wounded, it falls into the enemy's hands. The Roman soldiers rendered them useless chiefly by the following contrivance: at the instant the engagement began, they strewed the field of battle with caltrops, and the horses that drew the chariots, running full speed on them, were infallibly destroyed. A caltrop is a machine composed of four spikes or points arranged so that in whatever manner it is thrown on the ground, it rests on three and presents the fourth upright.

Elephants by their vast size, horrible noise and the novelty of their form are at first very terrible both to men and horses. Pyrrhus first used them against the Romans in Lucania. And afterwards Hannibal brought them into the field in Africa. Antiochus in the east and Jugurtha in Numidia had great numbers. Many expedients have been used against them. In Lucania a centurion cut off the trunk of one with his sword. Two soldiers armed from head to foot in a chariot drawn by two horses, also covered with armor, attacked these beasts with lances of great length. They were secured by their armor from the archers on the elephants and avoided the fury of the animals by the swiftness of their horses. F oot soldiers completely armored, with the addition of long iron spikes fixed on their arms, shoulders and helmets, to prevent the elephant from seizing them with his trunk, were also employed against them.

But among the ancients, the velites usually engaged them. They were young soldiers, lightly armed, active and very expert in throwing their missile weapons on horseback. These troops kept hovering round the elephants continually and killed them with large lances and javelins. Afterwards, the soldiers, as their apprehensions decreased, attacked them in a body and, throwing their javelins together, destroyed them by the multitude of wounds. Slingers with round stones from the fustibalus and sling killed both the men who guided the elephants and the soldiers who fought in the towers on their backs. This was found by experience to be the best and safest expedient. At other times on the approach of these beasts, the soldiers opened their ranks and let them pass through. When they got into the midst of the troops, who surrounded them on all sides, they were captured with their guards unhurt.

Large balistae, drawn on carriages by two horses or mules, should be placed in the rear of the line, so that when the elephants come within reach they may be transfixed with the darts. The balistae should be larger and the heads of the darts stronger and broader than usual, so that the darts may be thrown farther, with greater force and the wounds be proportioned to the bodies of the beasts. It was proper to describe these several methods and contrivances employed against elephants, so that it may be known on occasion in what manner to oppose those prodigious animals.

RESOURCES IN CASE OF DEFEAT

If while one part of your army is victorious the other should be defeated, you are by no means to despair, since even in this extremity the constancy and resolution of a general may recover a complete victory. There are innumerable instances where the party that gave least way to despair was esteemed the conqueror. For where losses and advantages seem nearly equal, he is reputed to have the superiority who bears up against his misfortunes with greatest resolution. He is therefore to be first, if possible, to seize the spoils of the slain and to make rejoicings for the victory. Such marks of confidence dispirit the enemy and redouble your own courage.

Yet notwithstanding an entire defeat, all possible remedies must be attempted, since many generals have been fortunate enough to repair such a loss. A prudent officer will never risk a general action without taking such precautions as will secure him from any considerable loss in case of a defeat, for the uncertainty of war and the nature of things may render such a misfortune unavoidable. The neighborhood of a mountain, a fortified post in the rear or a resolute stand made by a good body of troops to cover the retreat, may be the means of saving the army.

An army after a defeat has sometimes rallied, returned on the enemy, dispersed him by pursuing in order and destroyed him without difficulty. Nor can men be in a more dangerous situation than, when in the midst of joy after victory, their exultation is suddenly converted into terror. Whatever be the event, the remains of the army must be immediately assembled, reanimated by suitable exhortations and furnished with fresh supplies of arms. New levies should immediately be made and new reinforcements provided. And it is of much the greatest consequence that proper opportunities should be taken to surprise the victorious enemies, to draw them into snares and ambuscades and by this means to recover the drooping spirits of your men. Nor will it be difficult to meet with such opportunities, as the nature of the human mind is apt to be too much elated and to act with too little caution in prosperity. If anyone should imagine no resource is left after the loss of a battle, let him reflect on what has happened in similar cases and he will find that they who were victorious in the end were often unsuccessful in the beginning.

GENERAL MAXIMS

It is the nature of war that what is beneficial to you is detrimental to the enemy and what is of service to him always hurts you. It is therefore a maxim never to do, or to omit doing, anything as a consequence of his actions, but to consult invariably your own interest only. And you depart from this interest whenever you imitate such measures as he pursues for his benefit. For the same reason it would be wrong for him to follow such steps as you take for your advantage.

The more your troops have been accustomed to camp duties on frontier stations and the more carefully they have been disciplined, the less danger they will be exposed to in the field.

Men must be sufficiently tried before they are led against the enemy.

It is much better to overcome the enemy by famine, surprise or terror than by general actions, for in the latter instance fortune has often a greater share than valor. Those designs are best which the enemy are entirely ignorant of till the moment of execution. Opportunity in war is often more to be depended on than courage.

To debauch the enemy's soldiers and encourage them when sincere in surrendering themselves, is of especial service, for an adversary is more hurt by desertion than by slaughter.

It is better to have several bodies of reserves than to extend your front too much.

A general is not easily overcome who can form a true judgment of his own and the enemy's forces.

Valor is superior to numbers.

The nature of the ground is often of nmore consequence than courage.

Few men are born brave; many become so through care and force of discipline.

An army is strengthened by labor and enervated by idleness.

Troops are not to be led to battle unless confident of success.

Novelty and surprise throw an enemy into consternation; but common incidents have no effect.

He who rashly pursues a flying enemy with troops in disorder, seems inclined to resign that victory which he had before obtained.

An army unsupplied with grain and other necessary provisions will be vanquished without striking a blow.

A general whose troops are superior both in number and bravery should engage in the oblong square, which is the first formation.

He who judges himself inferior should advance his right wing obliquely against the enemy's left. This is the second formation.

If your left wing is strongest, you must attack the enemy's right according to the third formation.

The general who can depend on the discipline of his men should begin the engagement by attacking both the enemy's wings at once, the fourth formation.

He whose light infantry is good should cover his center by forming them in its front and charge both the enemy's wings at once. This is the fifth formation.

He who cannot depend either on the number or courage of his troops, if obliged to engage, should begin the action with his right and endeavor to break the enemy's left, the rest of his army remaining formed in a line perpendicular to the front and extended to the rear like a javelin. This is the sixth formation.

If your forces are few and weak in comparison to the enemy, you must make use of the seventh formation and cover one of your flanks either with an eminence, a city, the sea, a river or some protection of that kind.

A general who trusts to his cavalry should choose the proper ground for them and employ them principally in the action.

He who depends on his infantry should choose a situation most proper for them and make most use of their service.

When an enemy's spy lurks in the camp, order all your soldiers in the day time to their tents, and he will instantly be apprehended.

On finding the enemy has notice of your designs, you must immediately alter your plan of operations.

Consult with many on proper measures to be taken, but communicate the plans you intend to put in execution to few, and those only of the most assured fidelity; or rather trust no one but yourself.

Punishment, and fear thereof, are necessary to keep soldiers in order in quarters; but in the field they are more influenced by hope and rewards.

Good officers never engage in general actions unless induced by opportunity or obliged by necessity.

To distress the enemy more by famine than the sword is a mark of consummate skill.

Many instructions might be given with regard to the cavalry. But as this branch of the service has been brought to perfection since the ancient writers and considerable improvements have been made in their drills and maneuvers, their arms, and the quality and management of their horses, nothing can be collected from their works. Our present mode of discipline is sufficient.

Dispositions for action must be carefully concealed from the enemy, lest they should counteract them and defeat your plans by proper expedients.

This abridgment of the most eminent military writers, invincible Emperor, contains the maxims and instructions they have left us, approved by different ages and confirmed by repeated experience. The Persians admire your skill in archery; the Huns and Alans endeavor in vain to imitate your dexterity in horsemanship; the Saracens and Indians cannot equal your activity in the hunt; and even the masters at arms pique themselves on only part of that knowledge and expertness of which you give so many instances in their own profession. How glorious it is therefore for Your Majesty with all these qualifications to unite the science of war and the art of conquest, and to convince the world that by Your conduct and courage You are equally capable of performing the duties of the soldier and the general!

* An instrument with four points so designed that when any three of them are on the ground the fourth projects upward. These are extensively used today for antitank barriers.

www.ingramcontent.com/pod-product-compliance
Lightning Source LLC
Chambersburg PA
CBHW020517030426
42337CB00011B/436